FOREWORD BY ASHA J.W. HARDNETT

100 POEMS & POSSIBILITIES for HEALING

VOLUME 3

I0616418

LAURA DI FRANCO

Featured Poets: Melanie Barnes~Da Evangelist • Moody Black • Brigette Burton
Jean Voice Dart • Christine Falcon-Daigle • Lyn Veneziano Fry • Norman Gordon
Elizabeth R. Kipp • Dylan T. MacDonald • Francesca MacDonald
Melissa T. Maxwell • David D McLeod • Marquis "13 of nazareth" Mix
Parushka Moodley • Donna O'Toole • Diane Wilbon Parks
Natalie V. Petersen • Jen Potter • Rev. Dr. Karen Schuder
Sensei Timothy Stuetz • Dinahsta "Miss Kiane" Thomas
Lulu Trevena • Angela Valis

FOREWORD BY ASHA J.W. HARDNETT

100 POEMS &
POSSIBILITIES
for HEALING
VOLUME 3

LAURA DI FRANCO

Featured Poets: Melanie Barnes~Da Evangelist • Moody Black • Brigette Burton
Jean Voice Dart • Christine Falcon-Daigle • Lyn Veneziano Fry • Norman Gordon
Elizabeth R. Kipp • Dylan T. MacDonald • Francesca MacDonald
Melissa T. Maxwell • David D McLeod • Marquis "13 of nazareth" Mix
Parushka Moodley • Donna O'Toole • Diane Wilbon Parks
Natalie V. Petersen • Jen Potter • Rev. Dr. Karen Schuder
Sensei Timothy Stuetz • Dinahsta "Miss Kiane" Thomas
Lulu Trevena • Angela Valis

To Jude—thank you for that purple pen.

Dear Reader,

This publication contains content that may be potentially triggering or disturbing. Individuals who are sensitive to certain themes are advised to exercise caution while reading.

The opinions, ideas, and recommendations contained in this publication do not necessarily represent those of the publisher. The use of any information provided in this book is solely at your own risk.

Our authors represent cultures worldwide, and as such, there may be differences in spelling, language, and expressions. As a global publisher, we have made the conscious choice not to edit these nuances, so each chapter is authentic and in its author's words.

Know that the poets here have shared their brave words with you with a sincere and generous intent to assist you on your personal journey. Please contact them with any questions you may have. They will be happy to assist you further and be an ongoing resource for your success!

FOREWORD

By Asha J.W. Hardnett

There are moments in life when the page becomes sacred, a place where you can lay your truth down without rushing, performing, or pretending. A place where pain can unclench its fists, exhale, and finally say, "Thank you for seeing me." You are now entering that sort of safe space in these pages.

My first encounter with that kind of sacred space came as a teenager when I tried to end my life and survived. A teacher came to visit me in the hospital. She brought me two gifts: a journal and a copy of *For Colored Girls Who Have Considered Suicide / When the Rainbow Is Enuf.*

In those pages, I learned two truths that reshaped me forever:

My pain was not the only pain in the world. My pain still deserved a voice.

Both were true. And in the tension of those truths, a poet was born.

I've been writing my pain, my peace, and all my pieces ever since. That early encounter with healing through words eventually became my life's work: guiding others to uncover, heal, and walk boldly in their God-given purpose. As The Purpose Doula, I've walked alongside hundreds of women, students, and community leaders, creating frameworks that bridge pain and purpose.

Years into my journey with poetry, I found myself on stages in open mic spaces where poetry dissolved walls and softened the guarded. It was in one of those rooms that I met Dinahsta "Miss Kiane" Thomas, the founder of The InkWELL and one of the contributing poets in this book. She curates sacred spaces for youth in the DC Metro area and beyond through healing in the pen. I've had the honor of serving as a teaching artist with The InkWELL, witnessing firsthand how young people transform when given permission to write their truth.

Miss Kiane and I have walked alongside each other for years as youth-centered nonprofit founders and spoken word poets. Through those open mic spaces, I also met Laura Di Franco, the visionary behind this collaboration. Laura and I are kindred spirits, both deeply rooted in heart-centered healing work. I've been privileged to dialogue on her podcast and witness her artistry. We share a fierce commitment to transformative healing. So when Laura invited me to write this foreword and usher readers into this purposeful gathering, a collaboration of 25 poets, therapists, life coaches, ministers, healers, and brave souls willing to put their healing on the page while supporting The InkWELL's mission, the yes was easy.

This collaboration is brilliant. I've previewed this collection and worked through several of the exercises these healers have curated. I know this book is life-changing. These writers didn't just share polished performances; they offered their transformed truths, their sacred scars, their hard-won wisdom. They wrote from a place of healing, even if not yet fully healed, understanding that healing is a process, not a destination. They're trusting you enough to show you what wholeness looks like on the journey through breaking, not just on the other side of it.

Between 2020 and 2023, I was pushed into a new level of brave healing twice. Breast cancer. During chemotherapy, my oncologist told me something that changed everything: *Exercise,* even when I felt weak. Even when it seemed impossible, moving my body and actively participating in my treatment made a critical difference. I wasn't just surviving; I was choosing to thrive.

That's what this book is asking of you.

100 Poems & Possibilities for Healing, Volume 3 isn't just about healing. It's about the possibilities that emerge when we write about survival, identity, emotions, loss, and transformation. This is not a book you read passively. This is a training ground. An emotional elliptical machine for your heart. It's a healing experience, a companion on the journey back to self, and a brave village of wise poets inviting you into your own transformation.

After each personal story and poem, you'll find a writing invitation. Some of you will want to skip them. But I'm encouraging you: do not just read this book. *Use* it.

Pick up the pen, even when it feels heavy.

Because passive observation will not heal you. You have to actively participate in your own becoming.

This book is a mosaic: multicultural, multigenerational, multi-dimensional. Within these pages, some writers connect to God through prayer and divine guidance. Some to nature through imagery of water, earth, and breath. Some to ancestors through inherited stories and intergenerational wisdom. Some to memory through unflinching witness.

In a grief support group, I learned that grief is like taking pieces of broken glass and creating a whole new piece of art. You don't erase the breaking. You don't pretend the shards weren't sharp. But you gather them carefully and arrange them into something that catches the light differently than before. That's what healing does. It remakes you into someone who knows how to hold both the breaking and the beauty.

The beauty of this collection is that it allows both writer and reader to feel truly seen, not despite our differences, but through them. Our varied paths to healing reveal how vast and generous the territory of hope really is. What could separate us instead connects us to wholeness, freedom, and the courage to become.

I believe in God, and poetry has always been one of the ways God reaches for me. But healing is generous. It will meet you exactly where you are and gently invite you forward.

As you journey through these pages, I pray that you feel seen. I hope you feel the courage to name your truth, not just the polished parts, but the trembling parts too.

Let me offer you a few poems as your first doorway into this journey:

With deep love, purpose, and expectation,

Asha J.W. Hardnett

The Purpose Doula

These Ain't Poems; These. . .

These ain't poems; these (are) breadcrumbs
Life lessons left behind to help others find purpose
They're hush puppies
Savory bites used to cover my tracks as I point our paths towards freedom
Towards healing
No...
These ain't poems; these are therapy sessions
Intimately private public life lessons
They're wins
Losses and failures
They are warnings
Red, yellow, and green lights
For some, guidance
For others, directions
They are personal reflections
And invitations to imagination
So welcome
But don't just sit here listening
And reading like you expect something poetic
'Cuz these ain't even poems

Undiminished Value

One of the best feelings in the world is finding money
Doesn't matter where, as long as it's found, it has value
Trash, car, ground
Washed and wrinkled in the laundry,
Ripped, torn, taped, stolen
Well. . .maybe not stolen
But lost, then found
I'll take it
Its worth is not determined by its journey
We appreciate it fully
Allow it to fulfill its purpose
To purchase, invest, save, buy, trade, or give
It matters
Regardless of where it's been
Or whose hands it's been through
The Department of the Treasury sets its price, and we comply
Without question
So why don't you trust the value The Creator has set on you?
No matter where you've been
Or what you've been through
You matter
Jesus proved that we were worth dying for
As if searching for a pearl of great price
He traded His, to redeem your life
Who are you to question your worth?
To tell The Redeemer anything other than "Thank You"
Is ungrateful
The very beginning of God's Word says
I am made in the likeness and image of God
The same God who created the sun, moon, earth, and stars
Fearfully and wonderfully created me
So when everything is in question
Life gets uncertain

I remember that I am because He is I AM
Where I've been is a testament to the mercy
And Glory of God
It has been an uphill climb to realize
That my story does not devalue my worth
It just means I have a story to tell
A way to help you avoid the places where I fell
Teen mom, college dropout, attempted suicide survivor
Underemployed, isolated breast cancer thriver
An intentional being created by an intentional God
My worth is wrapped in His worthiness
All my failures, scars, flaws, and insecurities
Can't limit me
Because God is the author and finisher of who I'm purposed to be
So with boldness, I declare
I am still a child of the King of Kings
Put on earth to do i'mpossible things
I take pride in the journey because God is in it
I've lost and been lost, crumbled, broken and torn
But no matter where I've been
Or whose hands I've been through
I have undiminished value
And so do you

P.S. May you do the work, not because healing is easy, but because you are worth it. And when you reach those writing prompts, don't skip them. Your healing is waiting there, pen in hand.

Just in case no one has told you they love you, I'm telling you now: I love you. You matter. Your voice matters. And your healing journey matters, and I mean it.

If you'd like to explore more of my poetry, you can find "Broken" and 40+ other purposeful poems, prompts, and prayers in my collection *W.A.S: What Asha Said,* available at www.ashaonpurpose.com.

Asha J.W. Hardnett, widely known as The Purpose Doula, is a multi-published author, spoken word artist, keynote speaker, and life coach dedicated to helping individuals uncover, heal, and walk boldly in their God-given purpose.

A survivor turned thriver having overcome a teenage suicide attempt, profound grief, and two breast cancer diagnoses, Asha has guided hundreds of women, students, parents, and community leaders through transformative frameworks including PUSH to Purpose™, Affirmations & Conversations™, and Control + ALT + Delete. She is the author of *W.A.S: What Asha Said, Transfer Please,* and children's affirmation books that have earned her the title "Auntie Asha" among young readers.

She has performed and facilitated at various venues, including the U.S. Capitol, various Busboys & Poets locations throughout the DMV, and Microsoft. As Co-founder of Beauty Time, Inc., wife, and mother, Asha is deeply committed to serving high-achieving women and purpose-seekers who know they were made for more.

Her mission: to inspire one million women, families, and organizations to live intentionally, lead with legacy, and create generational impact.

www.ashaonpurpose.com
YouTube and Instagram: Asha On Purpose

TABLE OF CONTENTS

INTRODUCTION

If you'd asked me just a few years ago, I would've sworn I wasn't a real poet.

I still remember sitting in that classroom, a terrified kid trying to memorize Lewis Carroll's *Jabberwocky* and then standing in front of the class to recite it. My hands dripped with sweat, my knees shook, and my heart pounded so hard I thought everyone could hear it. That was my introduction to poetry—fear, shame, and a whole lot of performance anxiety. From then on, I wore the badge of "severe introvert" like a shield. It kept me safe, but it also kept me small.

Then came the analysis years—being told to dig apart poems until they didn't mean anything at all. What a waste. Poetry isn't meant to be solved like a math problem. It's meant to be *felt,* to stir something inside you, even if you don't know exactly what or why.

If only someone had told me that poetry could be medicine, that it could heal and reconnect me to myself.

It took me a long time—and a thirty-year career in holistic healing—before I found my way back. And when I did, poetry cracked me open. I'll never forget standing in a ballroom in Sedona with 220 healers, reading a poem I wrote the day before. My whole body shook just like that day in class, but when I finished, I knew something shifted forever. That was the moment I claimed the title of *Poet.*

Poetry became part of my therapy. I've self-published books, stood trembling at open mics with my crumpled little papers, and learned that even when my voice shakes, it's worth hearing. Every poem I shared helped me peel back another layer of unworthiness and remember what I'm here to do.

And now, here we are—*Volume 3* of *100 Poems & Possibilities for Healing!* Twenty-four poets have their own story, voice, and medicine to share with you. Every chapter shares a personal story, poetry, and a writing prompt just for you—because this isn't just a book to *read,* it's a book to *experience.* This collaborative cast of poets from all around the world dropped golden, sacred breadcrumbs of soul for you to follow. They grabbed my hand in the mission to gift the world poetry, knowing full well the healing power it has.

Take this book in hand with fierce curiosity about your Self, at the next deeper level. Be brave! Grab your flashlight and shine it into the corners of your heart. What's there to be felt will be part of your freedom.

I want you to know something important before you dive in: you don't have to "get" every poem. There's no test or right or wrong answer. Just notice what you feel. Notice when a line makes you pause, or when something stirs in your chest. Sometimes it only takes one sentence or phrase to shift everything.

Take a deep breath with me. You're not just reading a book, you're stepping into a circle of friends—a community of soul-driven poets who believe in the power of words to heal. They were brave enough to show you vulnerable pieces of their souls and to use those tender, sacred words and thoughts to show you you're not alone.

You're home now. Welcome.

With warrior love,

Laura

I'm healed, transformed
no longer in the storm
of old story.
Flying high with the sun
light beams from each pore.
What's in store
only the highest, truest
version of me
for all to see
for me to be, completely—
love-filled badassery.
A magic wand in hand
for each heart and soul
I stand beside.
I guide brave words
and finally know who I am.
Finally: I am that I am.

Chapter 1

Divine Guidance

How to Hear the Messages

Laura Di Franco, MPT, Publisher

My Story

"I'm not sure what happened, but every time I sit down to journal now, a poem moves through me. I feel like I'm connected to this thing that's way bigger than me, and it has a voice speaking through me. It's powerful. It's weird. Sometimes I look up to the sky and wonder: *What alien universe am I on?*"

After mentioning to a Brave Healer friend what happens when I journal, I remembered what I *used* to tell people.

"Everyone around me seems to have this superpower where they channel messages from the Universe or their guides. And they even know their guides' names! I have no idea who my guides are. Every time I see a hawk circling above, I know that's a sign to keep doing my thing, but talk to my guides? Why can't they speak up and be clearer? I'm ready!"

The Divine portal for me is poetry. And when I realized it, I didn't need to know my guides' names anymore. I knew I could enjoy a powerful connection any time I felt like connecting. My guides show me in the form of poems!

Do you know how cool that feels? Way cool.

I do feel super-human when whole, perfect stanzas flow from my heart to the pen to the page. And when they rhyme? Oh my, that turns me on! The absolute best moment, though, is when someone sends me a note:

"Laura, that was beautiful. I really needed to hear this today. Thank you."

That's when I know for sure that this thing I do with poetry isn't just for me.

I connect to something bigger, and when I do, it's for others, too. And that becomes this burning purpose driving me to sit my ass down and get still more often. The busyness of life is a choking paralytic. When I don't remember that the channel opens *only* when I practice the radical self-care my mind, body, and soul need to clear a path for that Divine voice, I sit frustrated instead. Frustration isn't a great way to write soulful poetry.

Many call this writer's block. I call writer's block bullshit. Writer's block is when you're caught up in your ruminating mind and forget you have a body—a GPS system for your soul-calling and soul's voice.

Writer's block means that you've popped out of that full-body presence and you're in your mind again. Your mind will stop you faster than anything! Don't believe what you think! Sink down lower and take a full, pelvic-bowl breath instead!

We all do this dance in and out of our bodies and thoughts all day long, but I prefer to stay down in my body nowadays. It's where all the magic happens.

Are you bodyful today?

You can try it now, in a few easy full pelvic-bowl breaths.

Feel your ribs expand in all directions with your inhale.

Soften everything on the exhale.

Arrive fully in this generous precious moment, down deep inside, where you have a powerful connection to every answer you want, every decision you must make, and every desire that inspires you.

Right here.

Right now.

This moment is your opportunity to connect to your Divine portal and receive the messages from your inner healer and wisdom.

Breathe.

The Poems

Stronger

I won't falter
My belief is stronger
than my doubt

My joy stew
thicker
than the fear broth

I take a bite,
have to chew
pay attention before I swallow

I taste the commitment of joy,
realize how easily
doubt shatters my worth

It slides down my throat
eager to be digested quickly
become part of me

I notice and pause
before I sip
I notice and choose

I place the cup back down
and ask,
"Is this true?"

I remember the game.
I remember the illusion.
I remember the rules of the
Universe.

The Law of Attraction beckons
The rule of love pervades
The truth of who I am ignites
again

I won't falter
My belief is stronger
than my doubt

I like the work and promise in
stew.

Nowhere to Go But Closer to Love

I feel the fire of hope.
It's something stronger, though.
A promise from God
to my soul. . .
"You're safe. You're enough,
you're light. You're love."

And I show up
day after day
making my way through the pain
machete in hand
and blast through the strangling weeds
constricting boa-like vines
to find the truth
the secrets
the final solution
to my ruminating mind.

I find my inner child
sitting there
unable to play
quiet as a mouse
sure she'll be shamed
if she speaks
not wanting to draw attention
better left alone.
My heart breaks with the ache
for the part of me
unseen and unheard.

Reaching for her tiny hand
I surrender
make a plan
to remember who I am
continue the work
of brave healing. . .

. . . not to understand everything
anymore
but to be present
with my heart,
not ignore the ache
of wanting to be loved
a little more.

She stood readily
willing to come with this stranger,
this crazy-ass warrior woman
who whispered, "It's okay. We got this!"
and flew into my arms.
The embrace lasted for a thousand miles.
Decades of pain
dissolved in milliseconds,
the love-light blasting through
every crevice darkened and ruined
by fear.

I cried with joy
whelmed by the love
I was finally able to let in
receive
be
melding totally with the part of me
who waited so fucking long
for the opportunity. . .
. . .patiently, kind, gentle
nowhere to go
but closer to love.

For My Soul's Sake

Jewels in the forest
catch sunbeams
and flicker crystal rainbows
toward my eyes

Caribbean blue skies
hold the sunrise
like a spotlight
setting the greens on golden fire

My pace slows
My inhale deepens
The silence fills my ears
The first cicada interrupts

I've seen the heron before
four-feet tall
taking flight
leaving goosebumps in his wake

Everything is a miracle
vibrates through each cell
The cell he sits in
a picture that begs to differ

Each step I place down
on the soft earth
each breath I get to take
reminds me it's my choice

For my soul's sake
I choose miracles
and ease my mind
through this gorgeous day

An Ode to My Writer Friends

I scratch my dreams
All the most important things
Down into the sacred fibers
Of my paper

The blank canvas receives
Thoughts, desires, imaginings
Chunks of heart and soul
And it's alchemy

I watch as my dream life arrives
Through carefully curated lines
One after another
Stopping time

Magic occurs in these little curves
No matter if they're seasoned
With tears or smiles
It's a spell

I cast them wildly sometimes
And others flow with purpose so intense
They singe the edges of reality
Leaving ashes

Carried away by sweet spring breezes
I realize I created exactly
What I asked for. . .
These are manifesting pages!

So I pause and breathe
Deep inspiration, trust, and joy
Rise to the surface
And out of my pen

I send it all up as my ask
I know it's given, and then. . .
All that remains to do
Is bask.

It's time to write!

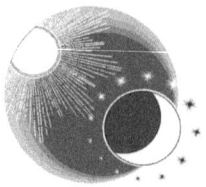

Dear Reader, now it's your turn to write. Use the blank space below. Try not to censor yourself.

Take a deep pelvic bowl breath and soften your body on the exhale.

When I connect to my inner healer and wisdom _____.

Laura Di Franco is the CEO of Brave Healer Productions, a 14-time award-winning publisher for holistic health, wellness, and business professionals with a mission to help the world experience what's possible. She's known as "the" publisher for healers with a 30-year background in holistic physical therapy and lifelong commitment to the journey. Poetry is her portal, a way to connect with a bigger manifesting energy.

Read more about Laura in the About the Lead Poet section.

Connect with Laura: https://lauradifranco.com

Chapter 2

I Invite the Stretch

Because Every Stretch Makes Room for Me to Rise

Melanie Barnes Mel - Da Evangelist, Poet, Entertainer

"True success is achieved by stretching oneself,
learning to feel comfortable being uncomfortable."
~Ken Poirot

My Story

I first tasted poetic expression in junior high school, where we had just embarked on the wonderfully imaginative world of creative writing. My imagination ran wild as I got the chance to express myself through the art of language. As poetry made its way to me, I left my feelings on the pages of my notebook like meditative prayers described in sacred texts. It gave my heart a voice as words beat from the center of my chest capturing every emotion and reminding me I am alive. I was smitten by her beauty and how she gave me life as though I had never learned to breathe properly prior to our introduction. Since that time, poetry has been my "waiting to exhale" on paper, a gentle reminder that I'm here and I am enough.

That my voice matters, and that poetry is the tool I use to plant seeds of prosperity. My words come back to me in multitudes of plenty, like fruit from a no longer barren tree. Sometimes it comes through with such clarity and precision that it lays out the passage in plain vision. While other times it evades me just enough to tease me into submission. I've learned to speak volumes with her permission. Even though there have been times when we've lost touch, I've found myself returning time and time again to see if we could pick up where we left off like old friends. To see if she remembers me. If she would still allow me to hold her with the highest esteem.

It had been quite a while since I allowed my voice to take center stage in my life. By the time I was ready to tell my story, I began to write, it flooded out onto the pages of my journal as though the levees had broken and being dammed was no longer an option. My story poured out of me with poetic elegance. I crafted line upon line with ease and profusion. Letting my truth speak as though it knew no other language than love. Poetry is the one that keeps me coming back repeatedly to experience its multitude of layers that catch me when I'm falling. It has afforded me the privilege of sitting in spaces that provided me with expansion beyond the ordinary. It's the one that brings healing on its wings and adds fuel to my dreams. See, poetry isn't just words on a page, it's my constant companion, my late night muse, my boo thang. The one who understands me when the world doesn't. There is no parting of ways; we belong together. So as long as she continues to show up for me, bringing gifts of beauty and safety, I will do my best to receive her with humility because I am grateful that she has chosen me.

The Poems

Code Switching. . .

I've spent the better portion
of my life trying to fit in

Instead of being
Comfortable in my own skin

You see, I got good at
Code switching, shit blending,
Twisting and turning and
Just simply pretending

All depending
On who was around
To see me compromising
My integrity. . .willing to be
Someone else's pedigree. . .
While the real me lived
Tucked away in the
Recesses of my mind
And my own life
I hardly recognized

And because
I was so damn traumatized
I'd lay my cultural practices
And urban vernacular
to the side. . .

Only to be reminded that
My ancestors had too much pride
To even consider laying down their lives. . .

But you see I had adopted the
Chameleon effect, code switching
At its best

And because of societal norms
And expectations
I mastered the strategy by
Altering my self-presentation
in different contexts and situations.

I even found myself switching up my style
Because I wanted you to feel more comfortable
With me around

Conforming to others' visions
Forcing myself to give in to their opinions of me

You see choosing whether or not to
Codeswitch is no light decision
Because the modified revision
That you present to others
Has to be fully convincing
It's an all or nothing decision

And that's where I thought
The magic would be
Living out someone else's
Definition of my identity

I told myself *baby girl, you're in a safe space*
But really I was just
cowardly playing it safe

Trying to be more palatable
Living only to make otters comfortable

With my isness, my blackness, and my queerness

And even in some instances when my femininity wasn't
feminine enough for you. . .
I'd do the most and switch up my voice too.

I played the pronoun game constantly
Where she became he
And he became they
And we consented to hiding and
Concealing never revealing our true identity. . .

I had yet to realize that I am
At my best when I'm freely me

At times it felt like I was wearing
an emotional straitjacket
Laced up into a version of me
That they found pleasing while the
Real me picked aimlessly at
The seams of my fragility
Cinching my voice so tightly
That even my thoughts
Became mere whispers

And because my mind was
Playing tricks on me
It had me subconsciously thinking
That if I could just get you to approve of me
Then that would be the thing to set me free
And provide me with the power
To do almost anything even if it meant
Compromising my own mental health
And self-esteem
By low-key allowing
You to shame me
Because for some reason
The real me wasn't good enough
And every move I made was

Being watched like I was under the microscope of inspection
For their correction and code switching became second
nature

It was as though someone had cast a spell on me
Forcing me to navigate between
Two different worlds. . .

So I began asking myself
How will I show up today?

By checking the barometer of my circumstances
I became an atmospheric meteorologist
Measuring the altitude of each room
I entered by the temperature of each individual
That didn't look like me

They say "trauma is cumulative over time",
Because the stress of not being able to be yourself
On a day-to-day basis
Decreases your window of tolerance

At first I saw it as no biggie
Until later I found out it was affecting me mentally

I was conforming to gain acceptance
Code switching out of necessity
With a constant balancing act of authenticity
In an exhausting dance with inferiority
While masking my identity and
Burying my feelings in a veil of conformity

Question: was it modesty
Or self-degradation?
Because in order for a spell to be broken
You must realize you are under one.
da evangelist

Roots ~ A Journey Home

My home was like a box
A container with no address
Just four walls with pieces of me piled high
Thrown in corners that knew nothing about the time
Or the care it took to create and
Erect the pillars of my life
Held together with pieces of my identity
A birth certificate, my baby blanket,
Several pairs of expensive shoes,
Many of my favorite things and a vault full of
Memories that no amount of time can erase. . .

And they I look just like my father

A house can't stand without a foundation
And a foundation is nothing without a home
When the soil is gone the roots have nowhere to roam
And my history was sold for pennies to the unknown
And absentee notes from my father was the emptiness in my songs
He was supposed to be the steel beams and concrete beneath my feet
But his absence was more like an infectious disease
that could of been cured with just a little stability

Instead he chose to do his own thing
Wandering thru life without really knowing me
Carelessly disposing of childhood memories
And you know kids, kids say the darndest things
"You can talk about my daddy, but not my mama"
Cause those would be fighting words but even sometimes
My mama started fights with words
Talking bout "you look just like your damn father"
And even tho my mama cuss her words still
Administered the same hurt
They should've been words that stirred up excitement
and make me feel good about myself

But instead they had the opposite effect

Maybe it was the disdain in her voice or
The pain in her face that gave it away
Or maybe it was the way she looked at me
Shaking her head in disbelief asking
"How is it you are not more like me, you look just like your father"

Taunting me with her words and making me feel like her enemy
I know she was only trying to protect me
Because a mother's love is not the enemy
She just wanted to pour into me unconditionally
But her hurt made her utter "Why can't you be more like me and your
brother? You look just like your father"

They say absence makes the heart grow fonder
Well my heart grew leaps and bounds
But just like puzzles with missing pieces
Your absence left a gap and was the reason seasons were misleading
Promising me warmth but delivering cold
And my untethered heart grew cold from the lies it was told
It receded gradually leaving me to believe that I must be the reason
Until grace gave me back the missing pieces. . .
Whispering, "You are not the seasons' reason" and
cleansed my heart of the debris that fell
From the lack of childhood memories with you.

And in that whisper I found the strength to go on
To reach for what remained tucked away in my heart
And we met at grace's bridge
Ladened with the forgiveness to mend the brokenness within

We dug through generations of barren soil
Planting seeds where love was soiled
And grace watered our roots while forgiveness ran deep

Then with a quickness I lost him again
Just when I got him back his soul took flight
And away he went along with the memories
of the possibilities of what might have been

So I was forced to rebuild again without him
But this time not with bricks or steel
But with the echoes of my father's laugh
The blessings from my mother's heart and
The strength of my own resilience to dissolve the past
And let go of what was once broken

And with that I rewrote my identity
Gradually healing each part of me
Coming to the conclusion that home is not a place
But that space tucked between belonging and grace
Filled with feelings of love that can't be erased by time
Leaving me with the feeling that even broken things can bloom

Sometime people don't live long enough to make amends
but by the grace of God, my dad did.
da evangelist

Labor is Love in Disguise

I ain't birthed no babies
But I have birthed a new version of me
It was the day my soul embraced expansion
And beauty disguised itself as defeat

With my fists tightly clenched
I let out a scream that split silence
As I broke thru overcrowded tunnels
Of traumatic experiences backlogged and filed
Under protective custody
Guarded closely by uncertainty and fear
Just to crown myself whole

At some point in our lives
We have to resolve within ourselves
Who we want to be

We must first silence negativity
And reprogram our minds to think the things we find pleasing
Because we are the architects of our realities

. . .and no it probably won't be easy

Because when something inside is being born
Birth in any form requires labor

Like when in labor
You hear wheels squeaking down
Long hallways of ceramic floors
Moving quickly beneath your gurney
Rushing you to birth's delivery, while
Passion thrusts down like contractions;
Pushing purpose through narrow passages
And becoming who you intended to be
Is hope's promise. . .

Life's midwife said you must trust the process
Because becoming is never passive, it's about
Remembering who you were
Before the world told you to forget
Before they fed you lies
So you would believe something different
Rewrote your history and played games with your intelligence
Filled your mind with deconstructed nonsense
Shawshanked your redemption and made-up facts
That wreaked havoc on your navigational system
And gave you an excuse to be less than the powerful being you are

See becoming is a labor-intensive care-giving system
That nourishes and defines stillness as divinity

In the stillness of silence your water breaks

Maybe it was a dreaded goodbye or a broken heart that ached
And left you feeling as though you wanted to die
But inside you lives a truth
Too big to unsee

So instead you decided to take life by the throat
And breathe in deep
But the air is thick with evolution's solution
So you push but the resistance is divine
Forcing you to see that you will only rise
To the level that you demand of yourself

So as purpose grows inside you and your life starts to change
You will begin to crave things that are different
From what you were once used to
Things that once felt foreign
Like silence over noise and peace over drama
No more noisy rhetoric, no more
Meaningless moments filled with distracting predators

As silence screams inside your spirit
You will resurface wearing a crown of redemption
That doesn't whisper but speaks volumes.
Can you hear it?
It announces, "You are no longer who you once were"
Now you are moving ahead
And with every step

you're bearing down on fear and ego's head
Now you're no longer negotiating with patterns
That kept you safe but small

So you remove the mask you once wore
And you forgive
Because you deserve to live
They say that growth isn't gentle, it's as harsh as truth
that it pulls ligaments of your identity
and snaps comfort at its root. . .

So now your navigational system is able to reboot
So when you replant, replant with truth
From silence that speaks volumes

Because when the new you is born bloody and breathless
Yet still alive there's a quiet stillness
A sacred holding
A simple knowing
That there is no enemy on the inside
That labor is love in disguise
And becoming, well becoming is simply the prize.
da evangelist

Wounds ~ Your words have weight

Sticks and stones may break my bones
But words will never hurt me
Lies. . .all lies. . .
That's one of the biggest lies ever told
Because often times thrown words
Hurt far worse than thrown stones
Cause thrown words tend to leave
Wounds exposed
See our physical wounds
Typically heal with the help of another
Remember it was much simpler when we were younger,
Perhaps all we needed was a Band-Aid, a hug
or maybe just a kiss from your mother

But when word daggers are thrown
They create invisible wounds
That heal with a much softer tissue
~and~
Every time another word dagger is thrown
The wound gets bigger
And ironically so does the issue.
So I encourage you to watch your words
When they're thrown
Every enunciation, even your tone
Cause with our words
We create life and death
With the power of our tongue
And with every breath. . .
da evangelist

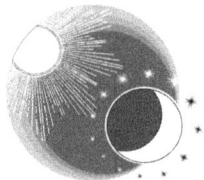

Dear Reader, now it's your turn to write. Use the blank space below. Try not to censor yourself.

Writing is therapy without the copay. It gives you the opportunity to express your innermost feelings, while providing you with a host of physical and mental health advantages that don't require a prescription. So take a moment to still yourself and go within. Embrace the freedom word therapy can bring by putting pen to paper where you will reap the benefits of self expression.

Melanie ~ Da Evangelist is a seasoned stage, film, and TV actress with over two decades of experience. With a rich background in entertainment, Melanie has captivated audiences in over 20 Off-Broadway and regional theater productions, earning notable roles in Roommates, The Laundry Room, and Lorraine Hansberry's *A Raisin in the Sun.* A five-year tenure with the New York-based Afrikan Women's Repertory, a recurring role on the Emmy Award-winning "One Life to Live," and NBC's "The Office" showcased her versatility on both stage and screen. Melanie's expertise lies in creating humorously nuanced characters with depth and soul.

Beyond acting, she is also a comedian, a passionate writer and poet, infusing her performances with the same humor and humanity that define her characters. In addition to her creative endeavors, she's also the owner of a new company that specializes in luxury bags and accessories that caters to the masculine-presenting woman who chooses to carry herself and her essentials in style. Though they're just getting started, they are committed to inclusivity and social impact, taking pride in their craftsmanship, and support of the LGBTQ+ community, with plans of expansion to provide housing for the LGBTQ+ homeless youth. If you're interested in finding out how you can support, please feel free to connect with Melanie through one of the links below.

Connect with Mel ~ Da Evangelist: https://linktr.ee/brnsmln45

Chapter 3

Our Kaleidoscope Full of Rocks

Writing Poetry with My Dead Dad to Heal My Soul

Natalie V. Petersen

My Story

A poet is. . .
     a lost person,
     a wasted spirit.
A poet is. . .
     trying to have feelings you can't find words for.
     If you could find words,
     it wouldn't be poetry. . .
     it would be that same feeling on paper
               for others
               to feel.
        The arms of love,
        the face of danger,
        the breath of fear,
        space,
        time,
        infinity. . .

Titled "A Poet Is," this scaffolding of words is from a book of my father's poetry that has been gasping for breath since placed in my possession many years ago.

The yellowed cover holds loose, chronological pieces of a young man's poetic mind. Turn the pages over, and I can feel the deep-dish servings of purposeful periods in the ellipses he liked to use.

Most of the book is typed on a manual typewriter. No fancy fonts, erase tape, or easy returns. Just one exception: a single line, gently scribed in light blue ballpoint pen, dead-center on the cover.

> *Read it from*
> *front to back*
> *the way it was*
> *written.*
> *Dad*

And so I have.

I have read my father's book of 88 poems, completed and signed in March 1972, just two and a half years before my birth, many times. There are typos and made-up words I've gotten used to as I honor his bravery over perfection.

"I string my words along this taughtly drawn wire of linear maturation and speak no lies and have no soul to hide. I am not afraid to allow you to view my thoughts in hope that you too may feel a little of my sickness in yourself," Garth tells you as we dive in, bubble-wrapping his deep, sometimes dark, innards with a delicately worded disclaimer.

"I began thinking about writing poetry when I was fourteen and didn't really feel as though I ought to. There came a time however, when I finally was stricken strongly enough with a mood to begin." The first poem in my father's collection is called "Truth," and it is an ode to his first love.

"Once finished with that, I turned back to the everyday life of the prodding small town school boy. It wasn't long before I came to my second expressional tremor," he goes on.

And on he goes. Courageously. Messily. He shares that the bulk of the poems were written in the last three of the six years it took to complete the book, which makes sense given the topics of war, sex, gnarly drugs, and leaving behind everything his parents represented as he struck out to find his own voice and free his soul.

Garth closes in a familiar, light, and philosophical air that I remember from even the deepest, darkest topics we'd share: "It is here I would like to tell the reader that my thoughts are for slow, relaxed reading."

Every time through, I've found a new thread to a new story. And here I am again, this time, sharing it with you.

The Poems

My words here aren't too scripted, folks, and at best, they're awkward. Yet, reflections on a careful selection of my father's poetry seem rather deliciously twisted and therefore perfectly suited for these pages with you. I wonder what we'll find in between the lines this time . . .

About Your "Suicide"

so you don't capitalize i
               but you do capitalize Man
and the standoff stayed stood up
                    'til little you done chased big Him away

how tragic your sweet fury
               demise delish
               controlled fury
your love was a far cry from lazy
               your absence made family

                                        tragically incomplete

i've missed the i, the capital Man
               the mind you say broke
mine has too
       again   and again, just today

you teach me now though
               preach through me now though

i recognize your i in my lines and my eyes now though
               feel the weight of your thumb in mine now

though i don't recall being in a place of such peace with your passing as now

your death was your destiny

and my voice is your legacy

i am Natalie
     my father was a poet
          a preacher
               and a charming, sweet man.

his steady hands were weathered
          and his eyes smiled creases so deep you could swim in 'em.

he danced up a dream and dances in my dreams still
                    i think i see now
                        how he split into two from one

and this is how we dance today
on full display

sad?

far from it

gay

gaiety

it's a thang

a state

your state when you're cheerful
lighthearted
free

some call it toxic
i've been called fake

delusional

a joke

we laugh regardless
we need your permission to live
as much as i need a Dad that shouldah couldah wouldah

stayed.

And "About Politicians"?

You said,
"If you think. . . . . . .don't."
and for years,
I held that line in my back pocket
like a warning,
or a wink.

Because you didn't mean *don't think,*
you meant *be careful.*

"Pain and agony come to those who think."

Shit, I feel it.

Not the kind of pain that cuts, but the ache that comes
        from caring far too fucking much in a world trained to numb.

I imagine us at the table you built me now
You, with your quiet sharpness,
Stubby pencil in hand, ready to write something profound,

And me, all open ribcage and messy, tragically optimistic. . . all hope.

And I wonder:

Where would we land?

Where would we stand
        when the votes are counted,
        the headlines neatly stacked,
        the truths untangled into one?

Would we . . . remember . . .

"Upon a pedestal sit those who don't think,"
        but perform so well, earning applause for pretending they can?

Would we both feel the weight

"but present the pain and agony to those
that do. . ."
and call it what it is:
    the cost of staying awake?

You always did have a way
of packing a universe into tight spaces.

Your words carried more than *discretion,*
they carried *knowing.*
I know how to carry *that* now.

And, I *do* think, Dad.
I think out loud.
I think often,
even when it's hard,
and especially when it's hard, Dad.

I am asking brave questions like you did, Dad.
And I am learning every day to sit with hard, not-so-easy,
sometimes very messy answers.
Sometimes I just sit,
because I have found that silence speaks very loud, too, Dad.

Maybe we'd sit
and see it differently.
Maybe we'd be more aligned than not.
But either way
I know you'd listen.
And I'd listen, too.

Oh gosh, would I listen.
I would listen to you.

Because in the end,
this whole messy *poh-lit-tick-uhl* thing?
It's an experiment we're in
and witnessing
being willing to wonder.

To think.
To feel.
To remember . . .

Seeing in exponentially faster time,
the cost of pretending not to.

I'll take your poem and your sweet, curious voice with me, Dad—
not as a warning, but as legacy, my inheritance.

A riddle worth solving every time the world forgets
what it means to lead with humanity.

The Weaving of "A Premonition"

by my father and me

Gaiety,
*oh, gaiety, ever real, or just paper confetti tossed into the wind of a lucky
window in time?*

by the ton
*church halls 'n' street dances, in the way we kids thought about school
without flinchin'*

or twice the ton
*we still build wild holidays out of it,
light sparklers and fire and flame up the name of it,
praying spraying joy and wishing grasping for weightlessness.*

or tons of tons of tons.
*some of us carry it as an inheritance,
for good and sometimes not so much,
and always, like armor, a sweet hiss or heavy kiss*

It will be soon
you felt it coming.
i think we do, too,
this slow, sticky unraveling . . . always
unraveling . . .

when gaiety will drown
in headlines and algorithms
and too many nights spent scrolling
instead of singing.

in tons and tons and tons of gloom,
it's heavy, Dad, and you weren't all wrong,

ne'er to be recovered. . .
but i have to believe it can be remembered.

ne'er to be believed. . .
and yet, i believe in the crack between what was and what could still be!

ne'er to be felt. . .
feelings still rise, Dad, even in rubble.

and ne'er to laugh again,
i laugh. quiet sometimes. far too loud when i forget to guard my joy, protected
in my bubble.

or swoon in things like throngs of love
and they celebrate love in protest lines and potlucks, Dad.
it's still here, just. . . . . .
rearranged. . .

to any happy end.
the end being the end is enough.
not all can or will be happy at once.
thank you for teaching me that, Dad.

Our "Question In Prayer"

Where to now, my God?
        where do I go?
        when will I be free?
You have put me in a society
and it has turned into a kaleidoscope full of rocks.

You have given me a religion,
and it has told me I am guilty
and cast me into Hell's circles of death.

Where to now, my God?
I ask that too
but not with the same despair.

I ask with a pen in my hand
and my ancestors at my back,
wild with dreams
they never got to live.

I ask
with breath still in my body
and a heart that beats in circles
not of hell,
but of healing.

where do I go?
Forward.
I go toward the breaking,
toward the loving,
toward the small moments

where truth slips through
and I have the guts
to name it out loud.

when will I be free?

Now.
Not all at once—
but now,
in the tiny choices to stay,
to speak up,
to feel it all
and not run.

Though holy fuck I've thought about it,
I have yet to actually run.

You have put me into a society
and it has turned into a kaleidoscope full of rocks.
And I sift through those very rocks now for roots.

I gather stories,
stack them like cairns,
marking the trail
so my son,
and his children,
and their wild, wondering hearts
can find their way home.

You have given me a religion,
and it has told me I am guilty
and cast me into Hell's circles of death.
And I have rewritten the doctrine
with questions,
with conversations,
with a gospel of becoming.

I found Spirit
not in shame,
but in the sound of my voice.

Not in rules,
but in relationship with my Self.

Not in Hell,
but in humanity, in community.

In Love.

My God, my god, my GAWD!
Mine is mine and mine alone.

My faith.

My own.

And so,
I walk forward—
not free from pain,
but rooted in purpose.

Not above the past,
but deeper into its soil
so I can grow something new.

I carry my Petersens with me—
every stubborn rib
and laughing jaw,
every poem left half-finished
and every dream
that never had a name.

I carry them
so my child can soar lighter,
so his babies can know
they come from people
who stayed.

Who tried.

Who burned bright and bold
with love
and questions
and a fire for truth
that didn't go out—

not even
at the last loving breath.

Tell 'em, Daddy, don't read me like a tragedy.
Yes, I come with ash under my fingernails
and loss stitched into the hem of my laughter—
but I am not what broke me.

I *share* the tragedy
so I can get to the triumph.

I *name* the ache
so it doesn't name me.

This living in the mess
and reporting from the flames?
It takes bravery,
and some days I just.don't.have.it.

Some days I spin and sputter and fucking forget what the fuck I'm doing.

Except to move . . .

Crawl . . . slither . . . slide . . .

With hope. Messy and hopeful.

Because even in your own disaster,
you taught me, Dad,
that my end wasn't in the beginning.

You showed me
that it's okay to fall apart—
so long as we keep gathering
the good stuff
in the rubble.

So here I am—
writing, unearthing, excavating
the stories you left behind,
the ones you never got to finish,

the ones I still hear humming
in the bones of our name.

So the next generation can dance
in our dreams—
like we do, Dad.

Like we *still* do.

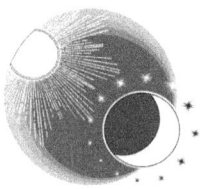

Dear Reader, now it's your turn to write. Use the blank space below. Try not to censor yourself.

This page is for you. No rules, no judgment. Just let it spill. Let your fingers fly, your pencil dance, your truth breathe onto the paper.

When you think about the legacy you're creating—what do you want future generations to hold in their hands, hearts, and stories because of you? Are you free to begin leaving it now? And if not, what one small step can you take today to start?

Though weaving tall tales and curating curious conversations since childhood, **Natalie Petersen** feels she's only just begun to unleash her writing for public expression. She has proudly participated in multiple bestselling collaborations, and opportunities to share brave words continue to grow.

When not writing, out in nature, or adventuring with family, Natalie is a mentor for misfits, the creator of *Healing-Curious Humans,* and the host of *Think Out Loud With Me,* a podcast where curiosity leads and authentic conversation follows.

A natural teacher, speaker, and community activator, Natalie thrives on building spaces where people can drop the masks, step into truth, and connect in ways that transform lives. With a storied background in media, sales, marketing, and mental health advocacy, she brings both edge and empathy to everything she does.

Natalie's focus now: igniting communities, sparking dialogue, and writing the stories only she can tell.

Connect with Natalie: https://1qr.com/nataliep

Chapter 4

Pores of Poetry

Drip System for Healing

Norman Gordon, Life Coach, Creative Writer

My Story

Poetry is one stranger you don't have to scrutinize to trust.

One of my favorite pastimes as a child was developing inner conversations. I credit this to my early introduction to composition writing and reading.

My interest in poetry grew as I got deeper into books. Different types of rhyming schemes and a variety of poems kept me entertained. Do you remember that time in school when no teacher was around? Yes, I remember gently knocking on the desk to words curated by me and my classmates, starting from second grade.

Poetry is a moisturizer of peace. It's that place with tools to facilitate every kind of emotion without judgment. Being a poet opens me to a deeper soul.

Life as a poet exposes me to the profound bond between humans and words. This encounter introduced me to useful tools a creative mind can take to any level of life.

The poetry arena is a come-as-you-are adventure. It isn't about perfect flow. It's presenting what's on your mind. Through allowing words to grow in their natural state, a greater level of appreciation comes out. This is an opportunity to say poetry is tolerant.

I've grown to deeply treasure my relationship with this art form. This isn't just another way to communicate with myself; it is a way to artistically express my mood to an audience.

Poetry is a natural healing concoction. It separates me from pain. Poetry is serenity on paper. The voice of a poet is a gem. The thought of poetry is discernment dialing recovery. This place is the most effective rehabilitation facility. The heart of a poet is soil that brings growth to the soul.

I encountered low points in life. As a teenager leaving high school, I was overburdened with figuring out my future. The disconnected relationship between my dad and me added to my frustration. In my first year of high school, he took me to reside with his brother-in-law, yet distanced himself. That time I really needed him. We reconnected, and he promised me funds to go to college, however he didn't deliver, so I discontinued my studies. For a couple of months, I struggled with a headache that seemed to be out of control. My relief came through poetry writing and reciting. Within a few hours of my poetic reconnection, a supreme home of comfort took over, making the headache history.

The shift you're feeling is real. It's a miracle for me as well.

This art form abundantly changed my perspective and shifted my trajectory. Great connections have been made with other poets since I strengthened my alignment with poetry. About ten years ago, I took on the name, The Poetry–man. I have created two poetry books (Island Thoughts Volumes 1 & 2). Volume 2 can be found on Amazon. Some of my virtual spaces hold the name, The Poetry–man.

This culture has become more than just words. The intimacy shared brings me out in nature to do videos. The exciting blend of video and voice tells that I have grown to love the echoes of poetry. My heart, physical, spiritual, economic, and emotional health are immensely served by the pores of poetry.

The Poems

Healing Mom and Dad

Sobbing dad
remorseful mom
consoling son
with flannel of words
cuddled by humane heart
barring guilty swords

The heat of May
welcomes an intense display
of 38 years of suppressed steam

Apparently, leaning towards anger
isn't the answer
No more making mom and dad strangers
myself a hater
because I was heated by him
and hit by her

An unchained glow
opened by the keys of healing
The atmosphere's caress
opens a flow, serene and captivating
Love, the medicinal jacuzzi
Breathtaking greenery crooning gently

Seeds of their needs
sown into my soul
saturate compassion,
forgiveness they behold
Protecting their conscience
from my youthful vent
is met by lenses of the present

Although soaked in remorse
It isn't about the past
It's bonding human gems
in comfort of family bath

Engaging in pure exchanges
rearranges messages
Minds moisturized and massaged
by notes from comforting chords
Vulnerability exhaled and inhaled healthily
Joy and hope excelled handsomely

Graciously glowing glee
gratifyingly greets gratitude
Precious poster parents positioned
for offspring to assuage painful altitude

Profound moment of endearment
I soon forget my own name
Retirement of estrangement
gives birth to umbilical attachment

Years of rejection
didn't outlive human lifespan
Sparks of humility and acceptance
attract admiration

From plight of loneliness
to flight of happiness
Three committed cheerleaders
spiritually bless the next aspect
of a chapter reset.

Growth Worthy

Ascension in progress,
regrets dismissed
Focus is the ignition switch
of purpose without limits

The leaf of life effect
One fall presents a thousand roots
Visionary beyond belittlement
sees fruits

Immeasurable images of creativity captured
Emerging ladder of a leader
Student of the student
Exemplary motivator

Life's increase on platter
in dining area of change
How strange to some
wisdom is a baton
The pass is perfect transformation
From triggers, rigors
and wound endangering

Arriving at the savory flow shows pluses
From pouring into a being
deserving of a scenery seen
as new beginning
Engaging in the rhythm of optimism
stimulates vigor, vitality and vim
Chaotic pain poses no restraint
when depth of passion solidifies gain

Both growth and merit
effectively work in pursuit of the truth
behind an existence consistent with high achievements
Here's courage with a cause,
faith in a vase
that demonstrates actions
in the why in the rays of the days.

Shift in Motion

Here's the shift
the gift, the music
Life, the unsinkable ship
floats with notes denoting happiness
Quantum hops on opportunities
Hugs on flights of positive self-regard
reaping and reaching reputable ripples
From boredom to boarding bountifully broadened horizons
Smiles are chimes serenading the sunshine

Days dutifully dance
and dazzle nonprogressive disturbance
Eyes aiming high,
hands hoisted
Heart rejoices to vision heightened
The gazebo of hope opens
to solve and fuel the mind
with deserved reclination

An era serving succulent beatific aura
Gems with undimmable beams of tomorrow
Hill's brow recovering now
Living in the version of an unbothered ocean
gives permission
to see waves of peace in motion

As senses cruise through spruce
at gate of eminence
imagination awakes breath
of growing paces
Echoes of victory grace the pavilion of joy
Ovation bids welcome
to the other side with wealthy supplies.

She Surrendered to Light

Clothed in innocence,
the essence of incense and blessings
Not apart from imperfection,
yet good-heartedness gave directions
There were turns and terms
when she learned how to navigate life
from the upside and other side.

It didn't matter who she sat beside,
there was something to take on life's drive.

A journey heated, sweetened,
frozen with a myriad of overwhelming flavors
Living, loving, escaping, surviving,
thriving was involved in journeying
The intention wasn't to be right or do right,
do wrong or be wrong,
but to be a good human

Not many understood,
though most should, her battles
She battled with,
couldn't say no,
couldn't let go
She battled with fear and insecurities
Self-compassion in limitation
Denying herself
proved to be strong

Could otherwise be chosen?
Yes
However, an overburdening cloud
prevented her from moving forward
Underserved ordeals
left her nothing to lean on

Bearing cuts, bruises, lies, excuses,
loss, failures, moments that damaged
Bearing the excruciating effects
of spears that smeared
The effect of not wanting those
who cared to come near
The effect of not being sure where you belong
Those broke a soul
that entered this world as a whole

She had clear goals
that paralleled her beautiful soul
Her hands were on the handles
before she was mishandled

During her plight,
she asked herself,
 "Am I getting it right?"
Though the predicament threatened her strength,
 she was aware of the more than enough length
in her strides to override
what was being battled internally
and on the outside
Thoughts she carried,
 "no longer will I be marred
by a situation that I seem to have married"

Consciousness rose higher
when she peered into the transformational mirror
and imagined brilliance behind sorrow,
success above brokenness
and a sweetheart
bigger than what was tearing her apart
The decision was to detox from all that went wrong,
recreate the great headspace
that had and still holds tools for happiness
A complete turn
gave her access to the excess strength she possessed

Scenes from components of history
that displeased and drained her
abruptly took leave
when she mentally left that page
to a version of light
that aligned with her values

Though there was no clue
when reality would be in full view,
She knew that a step
was a gateway to that avenue
Her follow-ups were fueled by self-belief
and attitude showing focus on her reach
As steps increased, though painful,
She hugged the appearance of envisioned radiance
Her past was relinquished by horizons attracting visions
She rose from under the cover
of what didn't value her
to being covered by what chauffeured and ushered her
to that kind smile
from the heart of a vivacious child
She rose to a taste
above testing nights,
tasteless days and painful fights
She surrendered to light

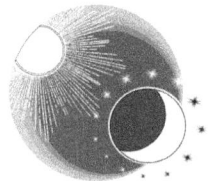

Dear Reader, now it's your turn to write. Use the blank space below. Try not to censor yourself.

How is your poetic emotion flowing right now?

Norman Gordon is a best-selling author, life coach, poet, and creative writer who hails from the fruitful district of Cromwell Land in the parish of St. Mary, Jamaica. He is life partner to his beautiful Abby, and a father, son, brother, and uncle.

Connect with Norman:
https://a.co/d/iYQ3Eb2

Chapter 5

Poetry as Therapy

The Benefits of Creative Self-Expression

Christine Falcon-Daigle

My Story

At 21, I graduated with a bachelor's degree from a small liberal arts school where I majored in English Literature and Psychology. It was the early 90s, the Cold War was over, and we watched the Berlin Wall get torn down on the evening news. America was at war in Iraq, and friends my age were enlisting in the military. I wanted nothing to do with that. I had big dreams of becoming a writer; however, poetry and short stories weren't going to pay my rent—something my hardworking single mom expected me to do, now that I was done with college.

I found a full-time job with good benefits at a local stationery store. I even had a 401(k).

My favorite part of the retail job was helping customers with the calligraphy and engraving services. I helped brides-to-be pick out wedding invitations, and expectant mothers choose baby announcements. But on my breaks and during my lunch hour, I read slim volumes of poetry.

Living in the Bay Area, there was no shortage of literary events. With over a year of solid sobriety, I wasn't spending my money at the liquor store; instead, I attended readings and bought books to have autographed by local poets Kim Addonizio, Doriane Laux, Kay Ryan, and Jane Hirshfield. I listened to poet laureates Mark Strand, Rita Dove, and Robert Pinsky read their work. I subscribed to *Poetry Flash* and *The New Yorker* and read each new issue cover to cover.

Robert Hass read at Lawrence Ferlinghetti's City Lights Bookstore in San Francisco's North Beach, where I stood wedged up against bookshelves, crammed like a crayon into an overfilled box, just to hear him read from his translation of the Japanese Haiku masters Basho, Buson, and Issa. Attending a dinner once in Los Angeles where Maya Angelou spoke was a peak life moment.

I will never forget the way these poets made me feel. Their words gave me permission to say things and express feelings I learned to stuff down and hide from others. Inspired and eager to learn the craft, I began writing lines and phrases on the backs of receipts, napkins, and random scraps of paper. I tucked these lines into my pockets until I found time to revisit them later.

I began submitting to local literary publications and entered a few contests. Sometimes these poems were published. I even won a few awards, which helped boost my confidence. I attended my first open-mic night and once or twice read my work to thunderous applause!

Poetry was a type of therapy to help me process life. At twenty-something, I was still sifting and sorting through my childhood, trying to make sense of a family that disintegrated just as I was learning to drive. My car and poetry were both vehicles that offered a type of freedom; discovering all the places they took me served as a great form of personal exploration—both of my inner and my outer landscapes.

The Poems

One Day

One day this will all be over
Whatever you're going through
Or resisting
Whatever you're feeling or not
Feeling –

One day, the endless list of things to do
Appointments to keep, problems to solve,
goals to achieve
won't matter in the least
Because, well: your life will cease.

When you reframe the game
you stand back, unable to
walk past a garden in full bloom.
You will stop and stare,
Admire the rise of the stalks
the 20-foot sunflower
Its face turned toward the source of its
Becoming, shining example of heliotropism

You will notice the patterns in everything
infinite tessellations and spirals
the way your beloved's iris shrinks and expands
The veins in their hands, the feel of your own teeth
From behind, the strength and softness of the tip
Of a tongue as it touches and licks wet lips

Wonder how you could have
Missed all this before? Feel more
Gratitude at the noticing, and soon use
gratitude as a portal to the present
You stop living in the future or the past
Make each crystalline moment last

Get that all this is happening
Whether we notice it or not
Why wouldn't we stop, drop
To our knees at the sight of our loved ones?
Open our hearts and arms to the prodigal
Child who had to leave on their own terms
Only to one day return
To their roots, where they were
first firmly planted in the wall
Of their mother's womb.

To understand how much
We are loved by God
we have to fall prey
To our own story of unworthiness
Believe the lies, that self-centered narrative
Used to distort and deny
The truth of who we are –
All stardust and cosmic light
Combined just right in an act of radical
Accord, superorganism of consciousness,
worn as an Earth-suit.
Society tricks us into believing
We are merely that which contains us.

We lose sight of the light
Within, we lose sight of the light
In others, we lose sight
Of the right to own
Our own soul, to claim sovereignty.
We must deconstruct then reconstruct
that early life experience called childhood
into a wholly new garment that fits like a glove,
A cloak of understanding and compassion
Instead of a hairshirt we believe marks us
As freakish, alone in our longing
To belong.

For even those among us
Who had picture-perfect childhoods
(as if there were such a thing)
Arrive to the battlefield of adulthood
Ill-equipped and questioning

We all wrestle with doubt and shame.
No one among us is immune from the struggle
This journey of life, full of strife, the desire
To find one's self, like it's some foreign identity
We have to work hard to uncover
Instead of our birthright,
the most natural place
In the world.

One day all the striving and
Jockeying for power will end.
I hope that day is long before
You take your last breath.
I wish for you a good death
In midlife, as the Irish proverb goes.
May the journey of a thousand
Miles lead you back to the home
Of your own tender heart,
The seat of your soul, your own divinity
Unprogrammed and pure,
unaware of and unbothered by
how long you've been apart
because for Her, one day never comes.
One day is always now.
One day is the endless cosmic stream
Of infinity, where she has been resting
And waiting at that still point in the center
Where the figure eight loops back
Crossing over itself –
The snake eating its own tail
In a ceaseless dance of creation.

Bless The Thing That Broke You Open

Bless the thing that broke you open
– the world needs us open –

Bless the thing that ripped out your heart
Ran it over with a cart led by a headless horseman;

Bless the knife in your back, its cold steel
Blade, that sharp spade that sliced your spine in half,

Split you in two, you an iceberg calving,
You, body limp on the floor begging for mercy.

Bless the pain that made you stop, slow down,
Look around in the burned-out house of your soul.

Bless even the bad dreams that woke you,
sweat-soaked and screaming, those night terrors and panic attacks.

They taught you how to breathe, how to weave between shadows,
Taught you not to fear your own darkness.

Bless them! Bless them all, for you would not know
Who you are—or how to survive—without them.

Qualified

How am I qualified to lead the life I am currently life-ing?
I have been midwifing my own soul for half a century now.
I attended the school of hard knocks –
Graduated top of my lower middle class upwardly mobile life.
Mom was a wife and school secretary,
worked at the Church, sold Avon and Tupperware.
I was aware from a very young age *I don't belong here.*
I was born to feel the rage my mother could not
certified in the art of feeling alone
certifiably insane at times perhaps
maybe just maybe top of my class *summa cum laude*
I wasn't allowed to talk about feelings
couldn't ask questions
don't cry or I'll give you something to
hang your hat on.
Got my diploma.
Got the letters at the end of my name
didn't bother to blame the failed first marriage on
not having parents who knew what love meant
who knew how to stay.
I say, I took up fencing
myself into little boxes and cages,
got late-stage anger, rare forms of depression.
I was raised by wolves, razed by the fires
that swept through our canyons,
buried us all under the ashes of secrets,
burned out basements, took the old house
down to the studs, smashed through the walls
jackhammered the cracked concrete slab
ripped up the stained carpets infested with maggots
feeding on generations of familial pain.
I got a degree in deconstruction, uncovering addictions
I wrote fiction—those lies that tell the truth
picked up my pen only to begin again
and again, and again

taught myself about dreaming
while life had its way with me
got a Masters in anxiety and panic disorder
once the weed and alcohol stopped working.
I rolled up my sleeves, got down to brass tax.
Thought I was having a heart attack.
Thought I was dying
called 911 more than once
met my own soul on the cold bathroom floor
begging for more, more than once
I talked about nothing, rambled to strangers.
The dangers of those conversations
rolled me like a dumb tourist
locked in the jaws of a croc
I was caught in a death roll but
I fought back
The nightmares were brutal
And once night terrors began,
I woke myself up often,
woke my husband, the baby, our neighbors
but I *woke up* damnit—no matter
how humiliating—
I got going, kept rowing my own canoe.
It's true and, in the end, I had to defend
the thesis of my own actions and choices
stare down the double barrel of the gun
I had loaded when my old life imploded
stare down the barrel of the gun,
locked and loaded, spin the chamber and
pull the trigger—*click*—still here.
With or without tears, I had to face
the music, the consequences of everything I had ever done
come undone like a tree in midwinter
stand there, naked and bare without flinching
Wait for the buds to begin breaking
wait without taking myself out
how I wanted to take myself out!

to hold my own feet to the fire
'til I expired, burst into flames and
erupt from the ashes like a phoenix
like that old burned-out basement
flooded when the pipes burst
there is no insurance money
there is no one coming to save me
That warranty, long-expired.
I had to get inspired
Face facts, stare back at myself in the mirror
only to smash it. My image shattered into
a million shards of glass.
At last, I held myself, both arms wrapped tight
Then, with all my might, pull myself up
by the boot straps
stand on my own two feet only to
find relief when I finally let go
collapsed in surrender, became tender
and finally forgave myself,
redemption, not graduation. What have I learned?
There is no title for the degree I have earned.
No finish line, no end in sight.
I had to get right with God,
tap into gratitude for the greatest teacher of all
the greatest lesson I ever got, I chose
through experience. It's the only way
some of us learn.
It's how I found truth, and choosing
the path of least resistance
without the insistence on doing
what everyone else wanted me to.
Yes, take and make with myself
something whole and holy, claim it
reframe it and start starring in my own story,
take center stage, turn the page on the past
look at long last, turn toward my Self
stare into the eyes of my heart

ask it that question
the only thing that truly matters:
Why am I here?
Allow it to answer,
listen to what I hear,
and then, find the courage to do it.

This Moment

Wield your pen like a saber.
Wear your softness like a shield.
Stay open, never hold the pain of others;
You were not meant to shoulder this world's suffering
Alone.
Let your body be a wellspring.
In silence, let the waters come in to renew you
so you can continue to give.
Don't try to live the lives of others—
You'll miss out on the one life you have to live.
Don't give so much of your soul you wind up in a hole,
Drained and depleted, defeated.
You did not come to survive, but thrive!
So, forgive yourself and rise.
Express! Put your pen to paper
Wield it like a sword,
Every word, deliberate.
Put your pen to the page
Wage war on the darkness inside.
Work that ink, let it go, let it
F l o w
Like a boxer in the ring
Rage against the machine
In the form of a sonnet, a couplet, a free verse
Lithe or terse
Float like a butterfly, sting like a bee, like Mohammed Ali

Free your mind from the confines of limiting beliefs
Who steal like a thief your sanity,
your joy, your peace, like Bruce Lee,
Be like water, let go, let the ink flow
From your pen like a samurai warrior of truth,
Like Luke Skywalker, shine your lightsaber on the page
Let your wild rage take center stage
Confront your own Darth Vader, dragons and tricksters
Those inner demons who want to silence and seduce you,
Who take pleasure in your pain.
Gain perspective, wipe the slate.
Paint over the old stories.
Purge, cleanse, declutter
Those closets and cupboards
The ones stacked with dirty dishes,
Old clothes, worn out and ill-fitting.
You're just sitting there, but don't despair.
Stare like a jaguar on the hunt
Gaze into the jungle of your dreams at night
Let your spirit take flight
Delight in the senses!
Your presence a present to all you help wake up
to this moment, and this moment,
and THIS moment.

THIS

Moment.

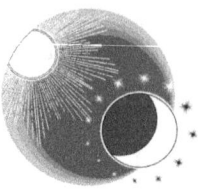

Dear Reader, now it's your turn to write. Use the blank space below. Try not to censor yourself.

Write a poem describing what you would like people to know about you, if you weren't too afraid to share. OR: Write a poem about someone or something you love.

Christine Falcon-Daigle is an award-winning author, poet, filmmaker, certified yoga instructor, women's circle facilitator, and transformational coach. In 2024, she founded Transformanity Collective, LLC to offer retreats in collaboration with other healing arts professionals. In 2024, she also became a founding board member and officer of Big Mesa Healing Sanctuary, a 501(c)(3) based in Marin County, California. Christine offers an online course on healing writing circles through Brave Healer Transformation School, and, in partnership with Compassion in Action and Solidad Correctional Facility (SCF), her course is available to inmates for free. A lover of the natural world and believer in the power of personal transformation, Christine has supported thousands through her work at the Hoffman Institute on a beautiful 200-acre property in Northern California since 2011.

Connect with Christine: https://www.christinefalcondaigle.com/

Chapter 6

Rewild

The Wisdom in the Rhythms of Your Natural Self

Melissa T. Maxwell

"We often forget that we are nature.
Nature is not something separate from us.
So when we say that we have lost our connection to nature,
we've lost our connection to ourselves."
~Andy Goldsworthy

My Story

My return to nature became a reclamation of my own natural rhythms.

For decades, I tried to measure up to invisible rules: how I should look, how I should succeed, how I should mother, how I should keep my cool even when I wanted to scream. I unsuccessfully chased other people's dreams for years, which led me to think, *maybe it's me.* I felt like a stranger in my own skin—outwardly grasping for approval, internally restless and numb.

It was nature that began to undo me at the seams. Not with a single strike, but with slow, steady unraveling to reveal the pattern hidden beneath.

The first time I hiked on the Appalachian Trail was the first time I paused long enough to hear the pulse of cicadas vibrating through the trees—a familiar sound living on the East Coast. My body recognized the hum before my mind could. This wasn't just noise—it was nature's rhythm. And in that moment, I realized: *I have a rhythm, too.*

The more time I spent outdoors, the more I noticed where my own rhythms were broken. While on a week-long backpacking trip, I started to wake naturally with the birds instead of my alarm. I noticed how the critters reacted to the full moon. I marveled at twilight, when the sky turned impossible shades of pink, purple, and indigo—a reminder that endings could also be beautiful beginnings.

Under the stars, old stories started to slip away. Stories insisting that worth comes from productivity, that stillness is laziness, and that beauty is defined by someone else's eye. Out on the trail—mud under my nails, hair tangled from rain—those stories felt absurd. The forest didn't ask me to be anything but present. The streams didn't care if my skin was smooth. And the hawk circling overhead certainly didn't wait for permission to spread its wings. *Why have I been waiting?*

Rewilding, I learned, isn't about abandoning life or escaping off-grid. It's about peeling back the layers of conditioning until your raw, untamed truth can breathe again. It's syncing to your body's natural cycle—waking, resting, eating, moving—in ways that nourish rather than deprive. It's trusting your intuition as a compass, the way moss knows how to grow on the north side of a tree.

And here's the truth I never expected: the version of myself I kept chasing through self-help books, expensive coaches, and endless striving wasn't out there at all. She was always here, waiting beneath the "shoulds" and survival. Nature simply cleared the way for me to find her again.

In the hush of the forest, I heard whispers from a voice I had long forgotten, reminding me that we are part of the great cycle, the rhythm pulsing through all things. When we align with it—when we rewild—we don't become someone new. We return to who we've been all along.

The poems I've channeled since are echoes from my aching soul—demanding freedom, peace, and connection. They weave a golden thread of truth: I am nature.

The Poems

100 Miles

My journey began with a single step,
into the land of birds, insects, and trees,
following weathered white painted blazes,
to breath-taking overlooks, down lush valleys.

Tunnels of mountain laurel paved the way,
as beams of orange sunlight dried up the path,
delicate white petals dusted the ground,
breezy green leaves shook off their dewy bath.

A steady pace drew me into my thoughts,
old stories arose to be rewritten,
my mind tip-toed into cavernous wounds,
plucking loose scabs I exposed untouched skin.

Gazing up through dense dogwood canopies,
crunching over pale peelings of birch,
its bark reminds me that I, too, can shed,
masks fall away in my ivy-draped church.

Loose rocks and thick roots threatened my footing,
presence tested by each little stumble,
mind seeking miles, body craving rest,
into streams my walls began to crumble.

The climbs burned my lungs, descents my poor legs,
pleading for the relief of level ground,
yet easy trails brought in harder thoughts,
torturous memories spun my head 'round.

Each day was a footrace against daylight,
aching feet and knees ready for retreat,
my empty belly grumbled as light waned,
a barred owl hooted away summer's heat.

I stirred from sleep to the sound of silence,
as dewy beads soaked through thin nylon sheets,
sunrise waiting for the raven's sharp calls,
taking first steps through damp grasses and weeds.

Dark clouds dimmed daylight for miles ahead,
prepared to wash away shielding lies,
in a muddy baptism rain showered
my rebirth in nature, I do surmise.

The thirsty earth soaked up the sky's waters,
fearless treetops stood up to windy blows,
I saw harmony within the fierce storm,
Pachamama teaching me all she knows.

Leaves of sassafras spiced the forest air,
I could taste the spring's mineral-rich drip,
both ears perked at distant coyote howls,
awareness restored near sharp as a whip.

Though I yearned to trace the path the crow flies,
gazing faraway hilltops of green hues,
I weaved on foot through steep rocky switchbacks,
to shed tears stood atop peaks I once mused.

What I thought was a long walk in the woods,
'twas really nature's initiation,
an embodied surrender to divine,
my soul's heartbeat re-synced with creation.

Out of the groves I return to safe hold,
with lessons the warblers and bees once told,
I carve a new rhythm from nature's mold.

Seeker

I looked through the telescope
searching for stars beyond reach
yet
all I could see was a single eye
of a woman staring back at me
she
who syncs seamlessly with the moon
following her sacral ebb and flow
trust
her cyclical dance brimming with life
body gyrating from her head to her toes
speak
her throat lets out a wild scream
beneath the noise, she recalls a familiar song
remember
her breathing unlocks a mysterious door
to a truth that's lived inside her all along
awaken
fourteen generations of grandmother teachings
forgotten recipes, song, and ceremony
listen
her ancestors whisper, *beloved child*
the galaxies exist in your blood
notice
her every breath is a constellation
stars are birthed, extinguished, then rebud
return
she crawls from the womb of creation
nursing from her deep well of pain
water
wildflowers who forgot how to bloom
and gather daughters to call in the rain
heal
with siren's hymn they resew torn hearts
weaving in echoes of elders from above
see
her eye was not a mirror but an open doorway
to a rhythm rooted in sacred love

Elemental

Dear reader, this poem is in a classical form of poetry called a sestina, where six chosen end-words repeat in a rotating pattern across six stanzas and conclude together in a final three-line envoi. The pattern creates a spiraling rhythm, mirroring the cyclical nature of the elements.

The seed from all we know emerged from love
A hum that echoed infinitely into space
Whispers that stirred the silence into air
Kindling to spark, combusting into fire
Warmth that dissolved into water
Appearing as sediment; settling into earth

The mountains hold steady piled with earth
Though silently pulsing with her love
The rivers carve her language out of water
Weathering stones to sand, commanding more space
Currents roar through the land like a blaze of fire
Dark shapeshifters of vapor in stormy air

The phoenix ascends, dancer of the air
Her shadow drapes softly over the earth
Eyes glowing flames, gazing with fire
She sings, overtures of resonating love
These harmonizing waves carried through space
She cries tears, healing drought like water

The milky moon rises over the water
Her silver breath drifting calmly through air
She draws the tides within her sacred space
Returning her blood back into the earth
Her ceremony an act of eternal love
Illuminating in her heart with fire

She transforms and purifies like fire
A medicine carrier mixing elixirs in water
Her caress creates trails of love
Breathing life into plants through air
Walking barefoot and covered in earth
Her visions born behind lids of inner space

Step into the vortex of time and space
Pour all parts of you into the fire
Feel yourself held by Mother Earth
Her rhythm flowing through you like water
Wordless speech spoken through air
Umbilically bonded by a sacred love

You are nature, sprouted from space, fluid like water
Metabolizing and creating with fire, alive through atoms of air
Your footing held by soft earth, and cradled by wild love

Rewilding

thirteen years behind a desk
perfectly prepared and polished
with Lisa Frank notebooks
and a fresh pair of shoes
first day jitters in my belly
how will I measure up?

thirteen years of striving
grinding through worksheets
tests and group projects
yearning for a "Good Job!" sticker
ninety seven percent
or bragging rights from an
Honors Roll certificate

thirteen years of abandoning
hidden dreams and talents
writing in secret
songs of unknown sorrow
words scribbled onto the paper
interrupted by thoughts of *shoulds*
silencing whispers of soul's calling

thirteen years of bells and pledges
but wait, it didn't end there
four more years
of competitive all-nighters
to be better than them
earn the piece of paper
and make someone else proud

well, funny thing is
you strolled off the paved sidewalk
treading onto the moist green grass
through thorny rose gardens
over overgrown weeds
you trimmed yourself a new path

for decades you stumble and fall
get muddy and scrape your knees
stuck in brambles
slipping on mossy rocks
tripping over hoses
and told, "get off my lawn!"

for decades you get discouraged
you feel like quitting, *why did I even try?*
but deep down in your heart
you know that you're meant for more
than to be a participant
in a race you never wanted to win

for decades there aren't any footsteps to follow
on a path that only belongs to you

no one to tell you your purpose
passions or preferences
so you feel confused scattered
and straight up tortured

for decades you go after shiny carrots
looking for easy way outs
implanted fake dreams into your soul
with elixirs of big promises
and stories that tease your mind
what do I actually want?

then you hear a muttering *listen child*
do not abandon yourself
do not settle for less than the dreams
that live in your heart
so you stop trading your years
for people places or things
that silence the soul you once knew

today you will be a student of life
rewriting roles and
erasing outdated timelines
once written a hundred times over
on classroom chalkboards
for punishment in a cage
that now you carry the key to escape

today you will see your light
peeking from behind the clouds
like golden beams of sunshine
catalyzing and transforming
a miraculous metamorphosis
into a beautiful butterfly
through pure dissolution of self

today you will remember
who you truly are
beneath countless layers of pain

spirit will exhale sweet breath
and seep through your cracks
breathing life into a still heart
restoring flow and intuition

today you will break down
dams holding in decades of tears
filling rivers with hope
courage to speak tangled words
waves pouring over the tip of your tongue
washing away old structures
smoothing the ground to begin anew

take your first steps
into this mystical wisdom
of stripping shedding and releasing
of ancient wisdom alive in your bones
and diving into the dark hidden corners
uncovering lost treasures of your soul

dear child
today you rewild

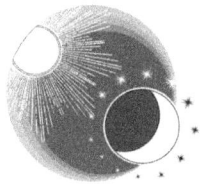

Dear Reader, now it's your turn to write. Use the blank space below. Try not to censor yourself.

What does rewilding mean to you?

In what ways do you feel out of sync with yourself or the rhythms of nature—and, more importantly, where in your life do you feel most alive in your natural rhythm?

Melissa T. Maxwell is a certified yoga teacher, holistic health coach, circle facilitator, and writer with additional training in embodied movement, energy healing, and Ayurveda. She alchemizes ancient lineages of wisdom with modern practices into multi-dimensional offerings that support whole-person healing.

Her mission is to help others remember their rhythms by rewilding their daily life—through seasonal living, ritual, and kinship to nature. Melissa believes that true wellness begins when we shed outdated stories, honor our cycles, and trust the innate wisdom within. She is passionate about creating spaces where women and families feel empowered to become their own best healers.

Alongside her work, Melissa is a homeschooling mama of two who loves traveling with her family, cooking nourishing meals, and deepening her knowledge while sipping a matcha latte. She carries a deep sense of curiosity, love for nature, and ability to foster connection wherever she goes.

Connect with Melissa: https://melissatmaxwell.substack.com/

Chapter 7

Believe in the Stars Within Your Heart
Trust in Yourself
Angela Valis

My Story

The salty spray in the sea air of the Scottish fishing village makes me feel crisply alive. Babe and I were finishing fish and chips with good friends. Warm cup of tea in hand, I muse aloud—"I love this hour each day; there's just something about it"—as my gaze drifts upward.

Nestled in my favorite café the following afternoon, I savor the sips. The aromas of coffee and pastries wafting by, the familiar hum of the espresso machine, friends immersed in conversations—I ponder.

What is it about my 'secret garden' hour each day that gilds it so golden?

Reasons become descriptive lines as I enter my own nook of a universe. For an hour, I ensconce, as I give words to my feelings and sensations. Rearranging lyrical lines, I craft my verse.

Upon arriving home, I tentatively tell Babe, "I think I just wrote a poem. Can you read it and tell me what you think?" He reads, confirms that indeed I have, and says, "Honey, you should send this to the local journal to see if they'd like to publish it." *Really?*

After typing it up, I attached it to an email to the editor. My finger hovering above the *Send* button for a solid minute or two, I wasn't doing edits; I was measuring my writing worth. *Do I believe enough in my words to give the ask?* I hit *Send.*

To my delight, I received a quick response. "That's lovely, Angela. I'll most certainly include it in the next issue."

Since then, I've written over 100 poems. Each one has given haven and life to a part of me that needed a river in which to flow.

This is what poetry gifts us. Poetry frees us to follow pathways to explore feelings, experiences, and fantasies. Poetry speaks to the depths of our souls and the heart of what makes us human.

Glimmers and touchstones present themselves to us most days. They may interweave truly tough times, no doubt. When we keep our eyes receptive to them, linger with them, and allow them in, if only for a moment, we're buoyed and reminded somewhere deep within of our strength and vulnerability, and that our life matters.

Poetry, nature, atmosphere, music, times with loved ones—all can help us to re-center and remember who we are at our core, and that which stirs and nourishes us.

The part of us that has dreams, optimism, curiosity, and delight, this part is still within you. All the deep yearnings and needs and desires, they're still there. And you deserve to have them fulfilled.

Oh, and that thing that makes you come alive and flow purely in the moment? Do it.

Trust in yourself. If your gut is giving you a "Yes," follow its call and see where the pathway leads. Believe in the stars within your precious heart.

The Poems

~~No~~ Outlet

What does it all mean?
What was I meant for?
    A glimpse. . .no,
            maybe not.

A ray of light. . .
    ah, well.

Tease me,
it's okay.
        Mess with me -
            what can I do.

We're all screwed
anyway.
        So why try, why
            follow the stepping stones?

Catch a break?
Not in this lifetime.
        The rules change
            every day it seems.

Ah, though,
there's that song I love. . .
        dare I let it in?
            to fortify me. . .

Why give my gifts,
    if no outlet exists?

But there's that song again ~
        it calls to that side of me.

A part that is brave,
        that craves,
            that won't be denied.

The ocean calls,
lap me up,
        rock me in your
            waves so warm.

The girl inside me beckons;
        she believes in the glimmer,
            in the ray of light.

That the good
        outweighs the bad. . .
            after all.

The sunlight of daybreak
        rises within our hearts.

We hold the key
        to thrive,
            to play.

*Let us now not just survive,
    but blossom.*

Picking Buttercups

The butter yellow
    caught my fancy
    from first days.

So whimsical,
    so feminine,
    so natural.

Small stones along
    winding creeks
    called to me.

Such gems,
    smooth roundness in
    my fingers,
    grasping for
    something certain.

Seashells speaking to
    my whimsy. . .wow,
    the world really does have
    a lot to delight in, after all.

So much more
    outside my door
    to explore.

Reality is better than
    I'd dreamt.

Of course the waves
    are still there.

Of course on larger stones
    my toes trip.

Of course some buttercups
    have missing petals.

Yet flowers give
    me hope,

creek stones remind me of
    my strength within, and

seashells assure we are also
    gifted fancy
    and bliss ~
    diamonds bejeweling
    our soft sand.

Sprinkling these along our
    pathways gently guides us to
    the light shining in our souls.

For these glimmers around us
reflect the gems within.

That Song

The experts say
scent is the surest route to
memory. . .

For me, it is
music.

With the first notes,
instantly whisked
away to when I
heard it first;
who was caressing
my face;
how I was laughing
or crying.

Enveloped deep in the
blanket of atmosphere,
feeling, and
wonder.

As Alice drifted down
the rabbit hole,
I follow the trail
offered for me. . .
a journey.

Will I allow myself
to receive, to savor?

From melody I
taste,
see,
smell,
touch.

Tasting nectar
for the first time,

delight filling
my being.

Seeing faces of loved ones
lost, but
living ~ by
lingering in my
soul.

Smelling honeysuckle,
glimpsing the tender
parts of me
still inside.

Touching the warmth
or coolness
of that moment,
nestling me.

The cradle of life
in which I dwelt during
that yesteryear. . .
abides in me still.

The texture of the threads
which held me then,
still strands within.

I am she, and
she is me.

As I meander round the
passageways where
music beckons. . .

Musings of the
melody of me.

North Sea Sands

I fell in love with the
North Sea upon first sight.

Wild, untamed,
cold, primeval.

Dunes carpeted in sea grasses,
kelp awash on the shores,
seashells and sea pebbles
adorning the vast sands.

Bundled from ankles up,
my feet freed,
soft sand sifts through
hungry toes.

Lining my pockets,
tiny shells nestle within
their larger brothers.
Tiny tidbits of eternity
resting in my hand.

Back home, I add my
newfound treasure to ones
carefully chosen on days of yore.

Perhaps I'll sort them by size.
They might love to be with
"their own."

Emptying a cerulean ceramic
of their sisters, the experiment ensues.
Now we're nice and organized.

Yet, trickling the same-size shells
back into the bowl. . .
left me empty.

These whimsical jewels cried
for their cousins.

For nature is neither
orderly nor uniform.
Flora and fauna refuse to be reigned in.

Nature thrives and shines
in glorious randomness,
untethered and free to mingle
midst secret liaisons.

Like a messy chef,
I gleefully mix the large and the small,
variety filling my fingers.

Ah, how will the bowl look now?

Into the ceramic go gems
tossed for eons by the waves of the world.

Imperfect perfection glances back at me.

Sea sand covering the table,
my seaside venture beckons,
"What about me?"

Sand sifting through my fingers,
innumerable sparkles smile on my skin.

Tiny crystals from the beginning of time
glisten, sprinkled with stardust.
The sands of time in my hand.

We are all made of stardust, they say.
Does my soul sparkle, as well?

Glistening gems adorn our souls. . .
let us savor the stars in our hearts.

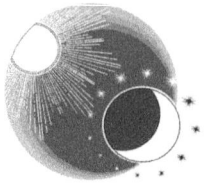

Dear Reader, now it's your turn to write. Use the blank space below. Try not to censor yourself.

What glimmers of curiosity or delight have been tugging at your attention? Might you linger, allow, savor for a moment?

Angela Valis is the author of the debut poetry collection, *Nectar,* to be published in 2026. She is a poet, flutist, and endlessly curious traveler.

Both as a child and an adult, atmosphere and nature have been portals for connecting with her essence, awakening her to wonder and discovery. More painful and conflicted encounters gave rise to existential questioning and a comprehension of our finite time on Earth. Later years provided perspective of her agency and what is of value.

Having invited back in delight, meaning, empowerment, and hope emerged, allowing her to not just survive but blossom.

Earlier in life, Angela was enriched by directing study tours for foreign officials, learning with fascination and empathy that the souls of those from different cultures do not differ much from one's own.

Angela's poems have been published in *St. Andrews In Focus,* Scotland, UK.

Connect with Angela: https://angelavalispoet.com

Chapter 8

Soul Spelunking

Descend, Illuminate, Heal, Rise

David D McLeod, DD, PhD, Certified Master Life Coach

My Story

I used to study faces like weather reports—always seeking approval and safety.

Do they like me? Am I doing it right? Try harder. Read another book. Ask another expert.

I kept moving, but a prickly hollowness followed me everywhere. Outward looked sensible, noble. Inward felt risky.

Keep it together. Don't make waves. Someone out there knows what I should do.

In 1995, my world cracked. Formerly reliable structures toppled. My inner voice panicked: *Fix it! Be stronger!*

One day, I sat down with my breath because there seemed nowhere else to go. In the soft stillness, my inner voice faded, and a powerful presence arrived—vast and intimate, like night air that knew my name. I came to know this presence as OMnitude.

"Stop scanning the horizon," OMnitude said. "Turn toward the lamp within."

"I don't know how," I whispered.

"Be curious; start listening. Ask one relevant question; wait longer than fear prefers."

That was the doorway. I began what I now call Soul Spelunking: a deliberate descent into my inner caverns, trusting my heart for illumination. It's simple:

- I sit.
- I breathe.
- I ask, *What seeks attention and healing now?*
- Then I wait.

Mental chatter sometimes distracts me: *This is weird. You're making it up. Better check your phone.*

I notice, I soften. But I hold the heartlamp steady.

"Nothing in you is the enemy," OMnitude says when I tense. "Everything wants to be seen."

In the cave, I discover ledges of sensation, stalactites of memory, streams of belief. A knot under my ribs; a picture of a childhood room; a sentence looping like a stuck song: *You are too much.*

I name what I find. I place a hand on my heart. I say to the younger me, *I'm here now. I won't leave.*

Sometimes grief floods, sometimes gentle relief.

Dear Reader
Being seen is medicine. When you do this, you may feel the hardest places relaxing under compassionate attention. No force is ever needed.

Over time, my inner blackness changed texture. No longer dank emptiness, but fertile loam that holds roots and supports life. I stopped auditioning for belonging and started belonging to myself. Guidance grew quieter and more reliable.

Dear Reader
You might notice this: a clarity that doesn't argue, a courage that feels persistent, a self-trust that lets you move without bargaining for permission.

Begin anywhere—a sigh, a tightness in the throat, a question you're afraid to ask—go ahead: ask it.

"Your heart is a lamp, not a judge," OMnitude reminds me. "Go gently. And go all the way."

Soul Spelunking hasn't made me perfect. It has made me honest. I still hear the old self-talk—*Hurry. Prove it. Don't feel that!*—but I know what to do:

Breathe. Look. Illuminate the crevice. And always listen: *What is true here? What needs care?*

I descend as needed, and each time I return with something worth keeping: a piece of myself no longer hidden.

The adventure continues.

The light is within—and it is enough.

The Poems

Here are four compositions birthed from some Soul Spelunking adventures—notes from the cave, written by heart-light. Each one commemorates a place I visited long enough to breathe, name what I found, and gratefully reclaim a lost gift.

May you be inspired to dive in, be curious, and trust your own heartlamp.

the mystery of me

here, i am this
there, i am that
a different mask for every occasion
a different persona for every event

these thoughts, these thoughts
    ceaseless and relentless
march like aimless nomads
across the ancient yearning desert
    of my mind

sometimes, they walk softly
sometimes, they dance on flying feet
sometimes, they trudge through mud and quicksand
    but always they move

  how shall i release them,
    these, my infinite children?
  how shall i surrender to the dance that is me
    and bid them adieu?

how shall i occupy the spaces between here and now
and still declare my essence?

as i move, i shift
and, shifting as i do,
i hardly seem to move at all

but only you
only you empower my smooth surrender
and witness my heart
through the translucent veneer
of my ever-expanding resumé

shall i join you there, among angels and trees,
where only gods and children play?

shall i touch you, at your heart,
and feel my own truth and compassion
beating inside?

if i disrobe
what lenses will cascade away from me
like so many discarded filters?

(oh, to truly see and be seen. . .)

as i shift, i move
and, moving as i do,
i hardly seem to shift at all

here, i am this
there, i am that
and in between, i am neither this nor that
but something else entirely

How Wise I Am

"Experience is knowledge with scar tissue;
Wisdom is knowledge with wrinkles."

Thus wrote a great sage whose name
Slips my mind at the moment.

I seem to have more of the latter these days—
    Wrinkles, I mean—
And into their deepening folds
    Fall ever more of my memories,
        Like hapless coins into a dark wishing well
        That never gets emptied.

As I age, my recall weakens and grows error-prone,
    Delivering memories I don't actually search for.
And yet (so I'm told), I'm becoming wiser.
    How ironic is that?

                    I don't have many gray hairs.
            My years seem to show up more
            As a soft middle bookended vertically
                By underused body parts.

                I don't look particularly old;
            I don't look particularly sage-like.
        Memories don't always come when I call,
    Or if they do, I sometimes don't recognize them.

And what is a memory anyway?

    A flicker of light across the night sky?
    A quickening heartbeat as a child is born?
    A waft of cloud drifting past the sun?
    A cool breeze in the middle of a warm day?

Is it light?
Is it dark?
Does it have a smell?
Does it have a color or a texture or a temperature?

All/None of the above, it seems to me.

Paradoxically,
A memory seems to have momentum
  Without any mass. . .

What is a memory, really,
If not a rusty anchor
In the ocean of the past?

Occasionally, I do remember clearly.
  I smile when that happens,
  And my inner imp does a little jig
  And clicks his heels!

Beware, World:

One of these days
I might just remember
How wise I am.

eternal truth

i am all alone with my eternal truth

i look into the beaming face
        of this innocent infant;
i discriminate yin from yang
and i see the sparkle
    of perpetual awakening,
even as the child
    penetrates, pierces
        my soul

someone

                            (over there)

    says

                god is a circle
                whose center
                is nowhere
                and
            whose circumference
                is everywhere

i am dizzy
    at the sensenonsense of it. . .
i thought i was paying attention,
but even the taste of the sun
cannot burn away my fear
        of being an illegal immigrant in heaven

i spin like a whirlwind of discordant music
    at the whim of a spastic conductor;
i twist like a kite wrestling with a hungry tree;

and the circle
absorbs me
into
all of its points. . .

somehow i recognize
    that a little miracle has landed on me
and i sense the truth of my eternal all-ONE-ness

the infant just giggles,
    as if there is a secret i'm supposed to know,
and looks back at me with
    big
        black
            godeyes

The Color of the Soul

I know my soul
Whenever I close my eyes and peer
    Into the dark place where logic ceases
    And only intuition exists.

I know your soul
Whenever I look beyond the surface of your eyes
    And let myself tumble into your depth
    . . .Without fear, without expectation.

What I recognize is
(of course)
Blue. . .

Brightblue:
    a song that dances on the waves of the sea
    until it is caught by a cormorant
    and carried to someone's lips.

Brightblue:
    the scent of freedom and truth
    that grows like downy hair
    on a baby's skin.

Brightblue:
    soft vibrations
    from the plucked strings
    of a finely tuned heart.

Brightblue:
    the promise of atmosphere
    that blankets me
    in an infinite cocoon of daylight sky.

Brightblue:
    the breath of an angel that sweeps by
    and whispers its truth
    through the fluteholes in your bones.

Brightblue:
    the long hollow spaces
    between delicious thoughts and dreams
    that follow an orgasm.

It's the only option, really, isn't it?
    Not red.
    Not yellow.
    Not green.

                No.
           Those colors just wouldn't
           Make any sense.

Dear Reader, now it's your turn to write. Use the blank space below. Try not to censor yourself.

Set a 15-minute timer. Hand on heart, ask: "Where in me is it darkest today, and what wants to be seen?" Free-write as if your soul is replying. Use "I" statements. When resistance arises, breathe and keep your pen moving. Close by writing: "One small act of loving care I can offer is. . ." and name it.

Bless you on your journey!

David D McLeod

Fighter pilot. Best-selling author. Software engineer. Mentor. Aerobics instructor. Poet. Janitor. Lifeguard. Musician. Radio host. Graphics designer. Father. Student. Teacher. Photographer. Ordained minister. Yogi.

These roles—past and present—add up to a LOT of life experience, which David McLeod brings to bear in his capacity as a transformational speaker, life-mastery coach, experiential facilitator, and writer/storyteller.

As a Certified Master Life Coach with a PhD in Metaphysical Sciences and a DD in Holistic Personal Coaching, David creates and shares powerful Life Mastery Tools that enable adult men and women to transcend triggers, challenges and obstacles so that they can express and experience the fullness of who they really are and thereby manifest truly magnificent and fulfilling lives.

Connect with David: https://linktr.ee/yourlifemasterycoach

Chapter 9

The Internal Rhythm

When Poetry Became My Pulse

Brigette Burton, Poet, Artistic Wellness Facilitator

"You don't have to be loud to be heard.
Your rhythm is already speaking."
~Brigette M. Burton

My Story

I had no idea I was wilting away until a poem whispered my name. I heard it loud and clear through the whisper, like moonlight slipping through a crack in the wall. It was so soft, but surely certain, illuminating the parts of me I thought were lost.

There was a time when silence felt safer than sound. My body moved, but my spirit lagged; it was stuck to pain, to memory, to a rhythm I no longer heard. I was only surviving, not singing, dancing, or living. Until one night, in the hush between tears and sleep, a line arrived. It wasn't written or forced. It just hit me.

It whispered, *Brigette, you're still here. And that is enough, my dear.*

That line became my heartbeat. I scribbled it into journals, wrote it inside my hands, until my pain took shape, until my breath had rhythm, until my blood felt warm again. It wasn't just a lifesaver. It stitched parts of me back together, one word at a time. It held me when no one else knew I was unraveling. It became the mirror that didn't judge, the quiet companion that sat beside me in the dark, and consoled the parts of me that burned inside, like a crackling fire unseen, but never extinguished.

Before I knew what healing meant, rhythm had already taken my hand. It found me in the sway of my hips when I danced alone in the bedroom, in the bathroom mirror, the bounce of my feet against the hardwood floors, the way my body moved like it answered a question only music could ask. Rhythm pulsed through me like the blood running through my veins, like a heartbeat, a secret language I didn't have to learn because it had always lived inside me.

By the age of nine, I awoke with rhymes already forming in my mouth. I recited my feelings before my feet touched the floor, like my dreams left behind little verses for me to carry into the day.

One favorite I chanted every morning before heading off to school went like this: "I'm going to be me, I'm going to be free, I'm going to be happy, just wait and see. You can't tell me how I feel, cause what I feel is really real." It's funny to me now because back then, I didn't have a clue how I put it together like this, nor its meaning, but I felt what it meant.

I lived between the lines on pages. They softened when I opened a book, and I let the rhythm carry me.

Poetry didn't tease me. It never asked me to be louder or tougher. It let me be soft and real. Poetry understood me. The words wrapped around my feelings like a warm shawl. They were a shield, a protective cover where I knew I was safe from harm. I didn't know it then, but I was building a survival system—one line at a time. Poetry wasn't just an escape. It was my blueprint for healing.

The Poems

The Rhythm in You

Pause.
Close your eyes.
Listen.

Not to the world's noise,
But to the quiet pulse
Beneath your skin.

Do you feel it?
The warmth of your blood
Like a river tide.
The breath that rises
Even when you forget to breathe.
The heartbeat
That has never abandoned you.
Do you feel it?
This is your rhythm.

No! It is not borrowed.
Nor is it broken.
And it's not too late.

It's yours.
It is ancient.
It is alive.

I found mine
In silence,
In sorrow,
In fear,
Then in the starlight.

I wrote my way
Back to breath.
Back to my body.
Back to who
I was supposed to be.

Now I ask you:
What rhythm lives inside of you?
What part of you has been singing
your world
All along?

Write it.
Dance it.
Speak it.
Create it.
Share it.

Let your rhythm
Be your medicine.
Let it be your map.
Your movement.

Let it guide you
Through grief,
Through joy,
Through the sacred remembering
of whom you are.

You don't need permission.
You only need to listen.
Because the rhythm in you
Is not waiting.
It's already singing.
It's already rising.
It's already ready to be heard.
It's waiting on you.
So, listen to your rhythm,
It will surely get you through.

Blueprints of Becoming

For every soul rebuilding itself from the inside out

We aren't born whole.
Storms carve us
and etched by aches
shaped by the silence that
follows every fall.

Life doesn't hand us ease.
It hands us edges.
 Sharp ones to be exact, ones we must climb,
That makes us bleed at times
and causes us to become breathless.
And still, we continue reaching,
To lift ourselves upward.

That wrenching pain, standing still
Like a sculptor —
Not to destroy us,
But to chisel away at the scars.
To reveal the architecture beneath our wounds.
To show us that being broken was never the end,
Only the blueprint of our truths.

I chose transformation.
Not because it was easy,
But because staying buried
was no longer an option.

I rose, not in one grand leap,
But in fragments. In whispers.
In the quiet decision to try again
when no one was watching.

Adversity became my teacher.
Obstacles, my alter.
And every scar, a sacred map
of whom I was becoming.

Now I walk with a different rhythm.
Not untouched,
But unafraid.
Not perfect,
But powerful.

Because healing is not erasing –
It's to be rebuilt.
It's choosing to see pain as a passage,
Not a prison.
And every time I rise,
I re-write the story.
Not of what hurts me,
But what I choose to become.
YOU CAN TOO!

Rise in the Rubble

For every soul rebuilding from the inside out

You've walked through the fire; you've knelt in the rain.
You've stitched your soul through many threads of pain.
The world once cracked beneath your feet,
And still you stood, though incomplete.

Each scar became a sacred line,
A map of where you dared to shine.
Adversity was your silent guide.
It broke you open, but not your pride.

You chose to rise, not just to survive,
to feel your pulse, to try and stay alive.
The will to heal, the strength to bend,
Became the path you learned to mend.

Obstacles came like storms at sea,
But you found the light for you to see.
You've built new thoughts from shattered stone,
And claimed your mind as a healing throne.

Now every tear, each sleepless night,
has shaped your heart to hold the light.
You see beyond what tried to break,
 those unique gifts in each mistake.

This life is not a perfect climb,
But every fall is rewritten in time.
You've risen in the rubble, bloomed quickly in the dust,
You now move through pain with sacred trust.

The Bridge to Green Peace

Where Earth's Rhythm Restores What Trauma Took

When the world bruises you,
When the silence
feels louder than breath,
Step into the green,
Where peace holds truth.
Let the trees say what you cannot.
Let the wind carry what you've buried.

Let the Earth hold you
without judging, without a rush.
Greenpeace is not just a movement,
but a memory of wholeness.
It's a rhythm of restoration,
a space for concentration,
a bridge between brokenness
and becoming.

The oceans do not ask us to be strong,
They simply reflect our depth.
The forests do not demand our story.
They simply offer shade
for us to focus
On our thoughts.

And in the quiet moss and moonlight,
The soul begins to remember:
We are not our pain, although
 it does cause strain on the brain.
We are not our past, because the past never lasts.
We are a pulse of possibility.

So, let the greenery rise inside you.
Let it soften the sharp edges.
Let it remind you that healing is
 not a destination. It's a return:
To breathe. To feel.
To stand tall through it all.

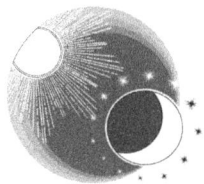

Dear Reader, now it's your turn to write. Use the blank space below. Try not to censor yourself.

Describe the moment when poetry became your pulse, altering your life's rhythm forever. How did this newfound passion shape your journey, and what challenges did it bring along?

Brigette Michelle Burton is a bestselling author, poet, artistic wellness facilitator, art therapist, and advocate for humanity. She's the founder of BHGS Publications, a soul-driven imprint devoted to transformative voices, storytelling, coupled with a gift for weaving poetic pieces into the technical intricacies of publishing. Brigette brings both reverence and precision to every stage of the creative process. Through her works of purpose and passion, she envisions a movement—one that empowers others to reclaim their stories of truth, to draw inspiration from others, to celebrate their voices, and to publish with intention. Whether she's guiding others through creative rituals, formatting a manuscript, or writing poetry to perfection, Brigette's approach is repetitive, intuitive, and joyfully transformative. Her work bridges poetic language with publishing precision, inviting readers into spaces of deep transformation, healing, and bravery.

Connect with Brigette: bhglitteredsoul6117@gmail.com

Chapter 10

Not So Perfect Ending

The Beauty in Letting Go

Dylan MacDonald

My Story

Fairy tales never prepare you for the real world. Throughout childhood, we're guided into sleep's gentle embrace by fantastical stories. They're fed to us like candy and referred to as gospel. These fables often depict a brave individual working hard to overcome struggles, ultimately leading them to a "happily ever after." Take Hansel and Gretel, for instance. The children, abandoned by the classic evil stepmother, find a witch's candy house. They push her into an oven after she nearly eats them and live the rest of their lives happily with their father; once he dumps his wife, of course. Regardless of how intoxicated the author of this fable might have been, this story always gave me a sense of hope. No matter the obstacle, whether it be a cannibal witch or a toxic friendship, it was always okay because it led to a happily ever after. Therefore, I expected nothing less after the arduous four-year adoption process matched my family with a beautiful little girl, one whose smile had me promising to devote my entire being to helping her.

However, life had other plans. The adoption, the supposed "happily ever after", morphed into a foster situation. After two years of dedication and love, my world was flipped upside down. It was no secret that my little sister functioned differently from my brother and me. She grew up alone in a third-world country, struggling to survive as best she could until an orphanage took her in and put her up for adoption. Long story short, her traumatic upbringing left her with scars we couldn't mend. We felt lost, stuck in a maze of sorts, unable to find an exit that would lead us to answers. We didn't know how to help.

For one thing, we realized we lacked the necessary tools to guide her through those difficulties. Despite our doting and love, she felt more alone than ever. I didn't want to accept this. Eventually, my parents made a decision: "She needs a new home, and will soon be departing from our household." There it was, the exit from the ever-compressing labyrinth, but I didn't want to take it. I wanted to be crushed by the walls as they closed in, more than I wanted to part from her. That changed when I saw her smile again, and my promise came back to me: *I will devote myself entirely to helping her.* Even still, my heart shattered into a million pieces, and I was left to pick them up, one by one.

In moments of despair, I turned to poetry, where writing became a cathartic experience. Ultimately, the fairy tales didn't deceive, for they were right in a certain regard: the trials are worth it. Not because they lead to the perfect ending we've been praying for, but because they shape us into who we need to become. My sister's departure was the catalyst for my journey into poetry, a path that has brought me clarity, a deeper understanding of love, and an outlet for releasing my deepest pain.

The Poems

Invisible wounds

If I could've chosen the torture I endured,
I would've picked one that was more obviously cured.
Forget psychological abuse,
Around my throat, instead, could you tie a noose?

I'd embrace the physical torment I deserve,
Watch the sheen of dulled metal hit a nerve.
Or maybe I could feel my eyes being gouged from my face,
The tears as crimson as red satin lace.

Maybe I could be skinned alive,
Or into a pool of sharp, rusted nails, I could dive.
Instead, this is the greatest pain I have felt,
Worse than having a broken bone dealt.

The blade that sliced my soul,
Along with the breath it stole,
Diced me like a tomato or fig,
Then, it butchered me like a poor little pig.

The sadness carved me hollow,
In this emotion, I would wallow,
For the solitude amplified it,
Loneliness loomed; it grew closer bit by bit.

Hospitals can mend the physical gashes,
But where was the ER when my insides turned to ashes?
Where were the doctors, the casts, and the stitches,
When the broken heart cast me into my emotional ditches?

But maybe that's why the pain felt so intense,
When you're left alone, all you can do is sense.
Healing sometimes requires picking the scab,
Letting the wound breathe, even if the cool air starts to stab.

Yet through the sting of the uncovered trauma,
Light will separate your pain, like a sentence split by a comma.
For a new layer of skin will start to grow,
You'll once again be whole; never quite the same, though.

Porcelain Mug

I'm too young for alcohol; for drugs,
For watching as whiskey fills my porcelain mugs.
I can't dull the pain the way they do on shows,
Take a pill or snort stuff up my nose.

I'm too young to wash back the tears,
To swish the liquid and swallow with cheers.
I can't have sex with the first person I see,
And hope this meaningless act completes me.

I'm too young to build a barrier,
Use these empty means as the emotional carrier.
But, maybe that's good,
These solutions are as fickle as wet wood.

What happens when the facade is erased?
When all the pent-up emotion is brought back, leaving a sour taste?
One wouldn't just be hungover from the booze,
But would also be trapped by the forgotten news.

So, it's good that I truly lived through the pain of a broken heart,
Experiencing as the puzzle pieces of my life fell apart;
For time is nobody's friend, ruling without compassion,
It will unearth the past with a ruthless passion.

I'm glad I watched as my porcelain mug shattered on the floor,
And stopped the shards from deteriorating more and more.
I was still in time to reassemble the bits,
Who knows what might have happened if I hadn't kept my wits?

The primal instinct to flee will try to save us from harm,
But being present in the moment is the charm.
Healing the wound before it could infect,
Allowed my sanity, for me, to protect.

Fly Away

The words didn't make any sense,
They swirled in my mind: Sharp; Intense;
The words couldn't be true,
For life couldn't just paint me that garish shade of blue.

Where was the warning?
I was left in the dust, depleted and mourning.
How could I ever regain my stability?
The rug was swept from under my feet, and I lacked agility.

It was as if an earthquake had shaken me alone,
Yet the decision was made; no plea could thaw a heart of stone.
The world used me like a tool,
Laughed at me like a fool.

I never expected my happily ever after to break,
It sent me plummeting into the frigid lake.
I didn't know up from down,
Now on the bathroom floor, the decision cackled like a twisted clown.

I heard a scream piercing my flushed ears,
It haunted me in the coming years,
Though it took me a moment to realize the shout was my own,
A wounded deer facing the unknown.

I looked down to see the sword that pierced my chest,
Though nothing was there, I was whole in the breast.
But what else could be inflicting me so much pain?
I squirmed and squealed; it was all in vain.

I convulsed as if I were having a seizure,
The wails, too big to be let out at my leisure.
Now a suffocating gulp was lodged in my throat,
The air expanded, causing me to bloat.

What else was there to be done?
I didn't want my sister to be taken by anyone.
But as the days passed,
It became clear that my parents' resolution would last.

How could they take my beam of light away,
And leave me drowning in my need for her to stay?
I felt like I was gradually dying,
Though my anger was misplaced, to myself, I was lying.

I wanted to hate more than anything,
To stomp my feet and scream words that would sting.
I wanted to yell till my voice went out,
And remain withdrawn with an everlasting pout.

But as the weeks approached the end,
The numerous reasons why she had to leave began to blend;
I started to understand,
The situation turned out more complicated than planned.

She was different from all,
Her past traumas constructed a wall;
She faced unexpected setbacks that needed attention,
Yet we had no idea how to lessen this tension.

We weren't prepared to accommodate,
We couldn't hide these problems away, like a broken plate.
So I learned to deal with the decision, even if it stabbed like a briar,
We put her needs over our deepest desire.

Though it broke me to separate,
And left me gagged and desperate,
I now realize letting go is the truest act of love,
Let them spread their wings and fly away like an angelic dove.

So Can I

It was hard to sleep, in the beginning, at least,
There was so much emotion on which my subconscious would feast.
As slumber found me, her face filled my mind,
Her smile was so innocent, so kind.

Then she turned and walked away,
I called out, but her path, she didn't betray.
I then tried to move to catch up with her,
But my legs were pinned, and my eyes began to blur.

The first night after my sister departed in that big, white Ford,
I was torn from one such dream, my emotions too strong to be ignored.
I sat up, the last discernible image of my sister's back,
Was firmly stamped in my eyes; my world went black.

My eyes were squeezed shut, but the tears still slipped out,
Flowing down my face, by now a familiar route.
The sobs were silent,
But these were the most violent.

I tried to shift the picture still lingering in my head,
But I couldn't change the channel, let alone go to bed;
So I sank back onto my pillow,
And did the only thing I could: wept like the willow.

Soon, the river stopped flowing,
But my feelings would forever continue growing.
By the time morning arrived,
My face was dry and somewhat revived.

However, for a while, things didn't get better,
At night, my pillow continued getting wetter,
For I realized something new:
Her memory of me will soon vanish, too.

Because of my sister's fraught upbringing,
Certain cognitive and learning obstacles were clinging,
Someday, this will cause her to forget
I bought her first doll set.

It's strange to love and miss somebody so much,
Knowing there is no reciprocation, not even a touch.
New dreams were added to the list,
Where I was overlooked and she ran to another, the one she sorely missed.

Cold sweats became a nightly ordeal,
To melatonin, I began to kneel;
Though in the morning, I was met with the same hollow feeling,
I tried to keep playing with the cards life was dealing.

As time crept forward, though,
I realized my funk had to go.
I forced myself to cherish our memories together,
Instead of mirroring ugly weather.

Through the tears, I found my way,
Re-discovering the beauty in each new day.
I realized that love transcends the physical plane,
And our connection as brother and sister would forever remain.

I now choose to honor her, for in my heart she will always belong,
She is a brave little soul who stares down challenges; she is strong.
If she can wake up each morning with a smile,
Then so can I. I'll just distract myself with the clouds for a while.

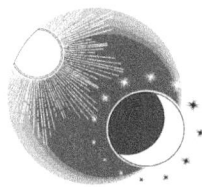

Dear Reader, now it's your turn to write. Use the blank space below. Try not to censor yourself.

Tap into your emotions and let your gut reveal what you're feeling—no overthinking. Capture that emotion on paper without explicitly naming it. Let your creativity flow and enjoy the process. Have fun, poets!

Dylan Thomas is a dynamic presence in the worlds of poetry and performance. He is a three-time winner of the Scholastic Art and Writing National Competition, having earned a Gold Medal with his moving poem "The Silent Promise" in 2024. As an elite All-Star cheerleader and hip-hop dancer, he commits many hours each week to rigorous training. His passion for movement is only matched by his love for K-pop music and extremely spicy Korean cuisine. Dylan's modeling career includes walking the New York Fashion Week runway for designer Mila Hoffman. As a high school junior, he is the editor of his school's literary magazine. Bilingual thanks to his Italian mother and American father, Dylan also speaks French and Spanish. His interest in mythology earned him a spot in Brown University's pre-college program. When he's not writing or performing, Dylan enjoys spending time with his cat, Nash, reading, and drawing.

Conect with Dylan: https://www.dylanval.com/

Chapter 11

Love Louder Than Words

Bonds That Transcend Oceans and Skies

Francesca MacDonald

My Story

Is there anything more meaningful I could do with my time than writing poetry? I often wonder.

The first time poetry flowed out of me was when I experienced emotions so deep they defied words. As a young adult, I read Jack Kerouac's *On the Road,* watched the film "Zabriskie Point," and decided to travel across the United States, just like Daria, the heroine of the movie. This was going to be my rite of passage into becoming an independent woman.

I told myself, *I got this,* my crooked smirk of confidence softening my sharp jaw. It looked like a simple task, but living in Italy without money and lacking internet access proved me wrong. Still, I persevered. I not only reached Zabriskie Point and traveled across the U.S., but I also answered a call of destiny.

The reward arrived on the last night of my trip. As I drifted through the intoxicating glow of Hollywood, the air thick with smog and stagnant sweat, an irresistible force drew me in. It was as if the universe whispered secrets only I could hear, guiding me into a dimly lit venue. There, amid the electric hum of anticipation, a band took the stage. Their charismatic frontman commanded the spotlight, singing with raw intensity, his gaze locked onto mine as if the world disappeared. "He is my home," I declared over the loud music.

Despite the sudden attraction that brought my husband and me together, I had to leave for Italy. Oceans apart only deepened an emotion that started bold and magical. Months felt heavy, causing my heart to swell with increasingly strong feelings.

As rational thoughts faded, the urge to release my trapped passion grew stronger, like steaming, sulfur smelling gases building pressure beneath tectonic plates. Desperate to express the inexpressible, my poetry erupted.

Later, I found comfort in this outlet when my mother, my best friend, died young and unwillingly from terminal cancer. Her illness devastated me, yet my love reached into the ethereal.

In the depths of piercing heartbreak, a resonant voice within whispered, *Death is but an illusion; we are eternal. Words are not mere sounds; they are potent spells weaving the fabric of reality, breathing life into our deepest desires.* Even when I spoke to those who passed, I felt our words transcend boundaries, keeping their essence alive.

When I pause amid endless to-do lists and wonder why I write poetry, I remind myself: *It's not my place to question who will benefit. Just heed the call.* My journey showed me that the ripple effect of our words stretches beyond understanding, yet it requires our active participation. The world would be incomplete without our poetic expressions, and the equilibrium of existence hinges on our collective creations. Instead of asking, "Why?" I now embrace, "Why not?"

As I put pen to paper in the poems that follow, I felt my muses' pulsing presence. My immense love for them nurtured my colorful world, and a feather-light breath brushed my cheek. I sensed an angelic embrace wrapping my aura with warm protection.

The Poems

Beyond The Red Velvet Curtain

In the heart of an alluring city, where chaos and calm collide,
Twisting paths shaped us, a future to decide.
Emotions crashed like deafening thunder on that quiet day,
Bold and blinding, in a theatrical display.

A sharp sensation left us breathless.
Words swallowed by intensity, sweat on our faces, relentless.
The wise within murmured when those signs appeared,
For if we slumbered, the vivid hues in our lives could have disappeared.

On a mild January night, Melrose Boulevard pulsed with electric life.
Tired streetlights flickered, casting shadows on shops, both thrifty and rife.
The air, thick with dust, carried a mosaic of trials,
From goods crafted with history, and sour denials.

Arcane vibes teased my eager ears.
Curiosity piqued as I embraced hidden fears.
The night, just waking, with mysteries in every fold,
Promised more than a rush, young stories to be told.

My thrifted coat, too bohemian for proper Italian's best,
Held tales of rebellion, like a forbidden treasure chest.
Dreams and reality blurred, merging into one another.
Was I asleep in my bed, crafted by the knotted hands of my grandfather?

It was my last night in L.A., but I still claimed the city as my own.
I owned every street as if it were the walls of my home.
The buzzing Hollywood Gig was my destined place.
I gripped the rusty handle, cold and smooth, a breath in my pace.

Inside, thirsty souls gathered, drawn by the moment's allure,
Pulled by the incisive force of something poetic and pure.
I inhaled deeply, magic exhaling from every pore,
A juicy moment for me, impossible to ignore.

I wove through the crowd, the front row, my race,
Like butter on browned toast, I slid into space.
The room cocooned, humming with anticipation's sound,
Ready to crack the dam walls, carefully built from the ground.

The red velvet curtain stood stoic and commanding.
More than fabric, a gateway, secrets demanding.
Smoke drifted in a seductive dance, teasing the senses,
Ephemeral and invasive, breaking my loose defenses.

As the curtain rose, a silhouette emerged in a swirling cone,
Erupting like lava, mesmerizing, as if carved from stone.
Like a Greek god, he stood, charisma flowing like a gown,
His gaze swept the crowd, heart naked, wearing no frown.

A warrior's spirit, choosing light over dark,
His heavy presence moved civilizations— a beacon, a spark.
The first note burst forth, impossible to restrain.
A magnetic field formed, a rhapsodic melody seized my tingling brain.

My heart, wide open, welcomed its master from the fight,
Safe, triumphant, eager for love's familiar sight.
"I see you in my shadow," the front man sang with power.
His smooth leather pants shimmered, his bare chest oozed, to all eyes, a flower.

He spoke in tones of vulnerability, transformation in a trance,
And, BAM, like dry logs to flame, a spark ignited at first glance.
Our eyes locked, secured, intimate and commanding,
In each other's gaze, our fates instantly blending.

No retreat, no escape, we collided like Murano glass,
Rare and luxurious, under heat, melting to a liquid mass.
The reaction transcended chemistry, a dance of molten art.
A masterpiece formed, a singular creation, never to part.

No longer the same, two souls once individual, now fused.
A smoky shape, swiftly cooling, slightly confused.
Transformation profound, no retreat, no definition.
A budding journey forward, an irreversible transition.

In the maze of change, excitement met the unknown.
Guided by intuition, fate's crystal sphere had clearly shown.
In those eyes, I found a refuge where my spirit soared,
A fresh spring, where a rush of potential could be stored.

He stepped down from the stage, farewell in his stride,
A choking goodbye that "hello" couldn't hide.
Though powerless, his eyes pleaded for me to remain.
Yet it was understood that the parting was just a temporary refrain.

A sour separation, to let the new take form,
To settle the changes amidst the wild storm.
His firm, moist squeeze, the tremble in his voice.
Promised a future where passion was our only choice.

New Chapters

I've pondered why we cling to 'happily ever after,'
When it should be, ". . .Then he drew near, their kiss sparked a new chapter;
Their love lighted the path for humanity,
And everyone rediscovered their sanity."

I ask, "Why not let our voices soar,
To unveil our true, radiant core,
In someone who lifts us, making us more?
Why not express the joys only a full heart can confess?"

Living in love's intoxication is where I belong.
Yet I've wondered for so long,
"Am I wired this way, or is it you, my love, carrying me away?"

No news compares to the delight,
Of your smile's glow, a heartwarming sight.
That shy gap between your teeth,
Warms my heart with every beat.

I journey forward with these truths held tight,
Building careers, raising children, setting anger to flight.
As I scan the scene with pensive eyes, open and keen,
Pink romance and red passion seem unseen.

So, my thoughts play,
Dreaming of a world where passion leads the way.
Imagine choosing a cozy morning with a mate,
Or skipping the gym for a spontaneous date.

Shall we explore new ways to make love enticing,
And redefine what we see as truly exciting?
How about new traditions, like "bring your spouse to work day,"
Or a Starbucks brew called "The Double, Morning-Glee Foreplay?"

New generations need to see,
That love is the key to being truly free.
Beyond media's pressure or fleeting trends,
Love's worth exceeds what wealth pretends.

Soon, they'll find that love gives courage to be bold,
Making us question tales once told;
It turns truths upside down,
Like, "No, when in love, a smile shouldn't face a frown!"

And what I wish my soulmate to know is,

"My love, through our glance and connection,
I see the most beautiful version of myself in your reflection.
Our fairy tale begins where others conclude,
Stretching beyond horizons, where new stories are brewed.

With each sunrise, we craft in our own way,
An ever-expanding love, not confined to a single day.
In our 'happily ever after,' we weave our lore,
A boundless saga, where love is cherished evermore."

Strawberry Meringue

I wake suddenly, ready to embrace the gift of another day.
Is this the last? I wonder, as time slips away.
What I thought was mine, ephemeral, already belongs to the past,
Yet I hurry, determined to cherish these moments that cannot last.

Mechanically, I serve, a frail facade of strength I wear,
With compassion ready to crumble under deeper scrutiny's stare.
The hours are running out, and I'd buy minutes with all my might,
Borrowing time, if I could, to hold her through another night.

A tear rolls down; today, a light grip holds my mother in the game.
Yet her hand is warm, I notice, quite swollen, but the same.
I recall, when it used to soothe my fears, for thoughts ran deep,
She kept me company when awake, redness in her eyes, until I fell asleep.

With its squeaky shutters halfway down, her hospital room, my sacred place,
A realm where time seems to dissolve, a space of grace.
The bitter, suffocating air pulses with vulnerability; a countdown draws near.
Families' destinies stand at a crossroads, their vision no longer clear.

I reflect, nothing from the memory bank feels like a mistake,
And nothing said, hurtful.
Recollections are vivid and hopeful;
Discussions feel complete, and resolutions, meaningful.
Seeing her new lilac Pima-cotton pajamas with a touch of lace,
I unexpectedly feel alive and free—my heart swelling from my chest to my face.

I observe the plant on the bare table, a blossoming flower's magic to share.
I brought her a sweet treat, a taste of spring, softening the mood, holy and rare.
I realize, strawberry meringue, never her usual delight.
Yet today, it's a token of love, my heart's true intent in plain sight.

The energetic opening in the expanse draws me in evermore,
My vision blurs, and my heart receptors expand.
It's a dimension in between where everything vibrating low
Breaks away like dry sand.
The experience is visceral, unapologetic, and oddly familiar.
Although I acknowledge, I am just a visitor here,
I do not rush or dismiss it as peculiar.

I let myself sink into the void of that timeless agape,
Bask in the nectar of existence's essence,
I kiss her moist forehead, brush her cortisone-filled cheek,
Nurturing the eternity of our coalescence.
Today, we build resilience,
Fueling for days when the embrace will feel empty and questionable,
And humble, begging prayers will attempt to keep this bond unbreakable.

We go all in, both with the silent understanding that forever is our pact.
While tomorrow might be bitter, today we express our gratitude—
An ode, a contract.
I sneak another bite of strawberry meringue into her mouth, barely open.
Her look of proud defiance gives me the peace I need,
For I know that now, her transition must happen.

I set down a nearly eaten slice of cake, no longer fit for an elegant bakery display.
And I hold a body whose warmth slowly slips away,
Along with all the things I didn't say.
Did I rush her process because I'm a coward who avoids feeling pain?
And where am I—in a dream, sitting at the edge of my seat,
Or standing in a cornfield, soaking up the refreshing rain?

The Little Bird

"A little bird told me. . ."
It was always the opening line,
A phrase that deepened in meaning,
As I grew over time.

In my earliest days, it was magic in a book,
A tale to stop my tears, with just one look.
A creature that could calm a stormy scene,
Or hush the clatter of life's loud machine.

As I grew, the bird brought news of delight,
Whispering secrets that made my eyes bright.
Wrapped in surprises, with ribbons and bows,
It spoke of wonders that only a child knows.

Then the bird learned my secrets, as if by magic,
Listening to my thoughts, both joyous and tragic.
I pondered aloud, "Is this bird a friend or a spy?"
For it seemed to watch me with a knowing eye.

Its purpose became clear: to escort me through life,
Teaching lessons with love, easing my strife.
An unseen companion, with wisdom to share,
Helping me grow with gentle, loving care.

Through childhood games and teenage tears,
The bird was there, calming my fears.
When parents were busy, and friends were few,
The bird's gentle voice always rang true.

As I matured, its standards grew high,
Encouraging me to reach for the sky.
It spoke of my strengths and where I could shine,
Guiding me gently, with love divine.

In adulthood, the bird became my guide,
A friend who listened, with nothing to hide.
It knew my dreams and whispered them back,
Helping me stay on my chosen track.

With time, the bird grew wiser still,
Reminding me of life's gentle thrill.
It taught me to cherish the present day,
And find joy in the simplest way.

The bird visited my children, too,
Spreading laughter, as if on cue.
A magical creature, with a mission anew,
Building connections, strong and true.

Until the day the little bird whispered, "I must fly away,
But remember, my love, I'm never far, just a heartbeat away."
In that moment, I realized the truth, profound and clear,
The little bird was my mother, always near.
Her spirit, her guidance, her love so bright,
Continues to warm and guide me, day and night.

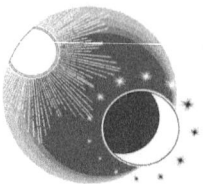

Dear Reader, now it's your turn to write. Use the blank space below. Try not to censor yourself.

This is your moment to unleash the power within and let your emotions soar beyond words. If you could express your deepest emotions without fear, what would you set free to elevate both yourself and the universe?

Francesca MacDonald is the co-founder of HitZero.com, the world's first sound nutrition platform, where users turn intentions into personalized Sonic Supplements™. An undercover poet since childhood, Francesca's talent for rhyming was first recognized in elementary school when she wrote a humorous poem in the Venetian dialect, which gained her popularity. Her love for poetry deepened when her muse, her husband of nearly 24 years, inspired her to write regularly.

A devoted mother, Francesca is committed to instilling a can-do attitude in her two boys and encouraging them to follow their dreams. She balances her career and creative interests with daily workouts, learning blockchain technology, and listening to engaging podcasts while ironing the family's clothes. Often found sipping cappuccinos with her miniature poodle, Oona, Francesca cherishes life's sweet moments with gratitude.

Her work has appeared in several Brave Healer Productions books, with more forthcoming.

Connect with Francesca: https://FrancescaMacDonald.com

Chapter 12

Reclamation at the Altar of Life

A Voice Uncaged: Poems for the Brave and Passionate

Lulu Pearl Trevena, Artist, Coach, Retreat Leader

My Story

I waited patiently to be introduced. One of the women in our networking group leaned forward and asked, "Do you ever feel nervous beforehand?"

I stepped forward after being introduced and addressed her question sincerely, speaking to all the women gathered for the luncheon.

"I've come a long way since this happened." I paused, eyes meeting theirs, now fully present center stage. "Picture this, primary school in Australia, what you call elementary school here. I'm about seven years old."

"The whole school is in the assembly hall, gathered to see a famous sportsman. The air is electric with excitement."

"I feel squashed, uncomfortable on the floor. I stand, asking the children beside me to make a little room."

"And then—out of nowhere—a booming male voice thunders over the speaker system: 'You. . .button your lip!'"

All eyes bury me by their weight!

The women's faces shift as they feel the heaviness of that moment. Hands rise instinctively to hearts, mine does too, as if to soothe that small girl still inside.

"You can imagine," I continued, my voice softer, "having the entire school's attention drop on me like that? It was overwhelming. Humiliating."

I stroll smoothly across the space with confidence, "To answer the question, *do I feel nervous beforehand,* yes, and I see how far I have come." Smiles and nods are generous. Still, vulnerability waits for no one.

In the last poetry collaboration, *Volume 2,* a celebratory open mic night was held at Busboys and Poets in Maryland. Though I was a collaborative poet in *Volume 1* also, this was my first open mic, and first-time reading poetry to a live audience. I've spoken on stage before, but not with my poetry, which feels like standing naked: tender, exposed, emotional, and honourably true.

That's what poetry is for me—raw truth, gentle audacity, and a reaching toward the edge of what aches to be named.

The MC introduced me after KaNikki, who proudly spelled her name a few times. On her coattails, with a little sass, I introduced myself, then leaned into the mic, "L. . .U. . .L. . .U," and added, "I'm Australian, I hope you can understand me." Laughter and warmth followed.

But it didn't ease me. I feared they now expected humour or lightness, and my poem wasn't that. My body felt clammy, perspiration trailing under my thick red curls, down my neck, even between my toes, of all places to notice. I felt faint and held the mic stand. I pep-talked myself through: *Breathe, pause, don't faint.*

There's a line in my poem: *you still shake with fear.* I lifted my arm so all could see the shaking. They may have thought it was theatrical. It wasn't. It was real.

The poem was well received. Many lines resonated deeply. I've included it here as my first poem; the performance is on YouTube.

Each time I step on stage, I meet my humanness—vulnerability hand in hand with courage. I uncage my words naturally from heart to pen to paper easy enough, and create an altar of a soulful lived life. My poems carry their own essence. Others hear themselves in them. Our words can heal.

The Poems

Like a Howl Without a Leash

Embodied:
A Feminine Return to Truth-Your Voice-Your Roar-Your Sacred Rise

women have suffered greatly
by being the "good girl"
locked in the looping program
of people-pleasing
let's get real:
healing from this isn't polished
it's not just soothing baths
confident no's
and glowing skin
it's messy
it's trembling lips
and a voice that still falters
it's finally saying *what you needed to say*
but afterward
shaking so hard
you wonder if you're falling apart
you're not
you're coming home
this is what reclamation looks like. . .
you speak the truth
that you were taught to silence
you cry the tears
you were told made you *too sensitive*
you feel anger rise (white hot)
not to hurt
but to clear
to burn through
and sometimes
you hold back

STILL
even after all the work
the therapy
the healing circles
the journaling
you find yourself
swallowing your tone
backtracking
and doubting your worth
because the old grooves
run deep
that's not failure
that's *integration*
so, hear this, love
there will be days
you still shake with fear
your voice will sound small
you'll want to retreat
to return to the safety of
easygoing
nice
quiet
but there's something **BIGGER** stirring now
something primal
can you feel her?
the part of you
that is done performing
the part
that remembers
the sound of her own *roar*
this healing isn't just about boundaries
it's about **unbinding**
unleashing the *you*
that was buried beneath
approval and appeasement
the wild you
the wise you

the embodied truth that pulses just beneath your skin
and yes
it may start as a whisper
but eventually, you'll feel it rise
the scream!
the one that's lived in your belly
since you were five
and told to smile through your tears
that one!
the one you've swallowed
every time you said yes
when you meant *fuck no*
the one you've buried
beneath the careful scripts
of likability and *should!*
give it space
a sacred terrain within
go primal
feel the low, guttural growl from the deep cave of your belly
S C R E A M !
scream into the ocean's wild edge

let your body tremble
let your voice crack and shatter
let your heart split wide open
all the way

O P E N

in Power

this is holy

this is alchemy
because behind the scream
is your **resonance**
your most authentic voice

liberated
and when she comes through. . .
you'll know her
she won't ask permission
she won't fit in a box
she won't be controlled
she is not a brand of empowerment
she is ***embodied power***

raw

sacred

sovereign
and even though this journey is uniquely yours—
even though no one can walk it for you—
you are not alone
there are others
quietly and bravely
doing the same tender, raw, unraveling work
there are others who will not look away
when you shake
or sob
or rage
there are others who will rise beside you
saying
me, too
keep going
when your truth quivers into the air
and that. . .that circle of truth-tellers and fierce-hearted feelers
can be one of the greatest blessings of all
so let this be your reminder. . .
your voice isn't too much
your truth isn't too loud
your no isn't unkind
your pleasure isn't shameful
your presence isn't negotiable
you were not born to be manageable
you were born to be
FREELY   YOURSELF

keep going
speak
even when your voice shakes
take up space
even when it feels unfamiliar
let the primal
become your *praise* song
let your truth live
not just in words
but in your hips
your breath
your spine
your yoni
your gaze
let the roar rise
fully feminine
inner-powered

and don't apologize
for the magnificence that is YOU
the real that is You
the fullness that is You
the heart that beats in You
strong
proud
sincere
whole
no more people-pleasing
YOU move through this life evocatively
a woman in sacred devotion
to the truth that bears fruit in her sacred body
love note: this is not mere poetry---it's a battle cry lit with wildfire, etched in
scars and stardust; a luscious homecoming, fierce and unapologetically whole

and I believe our ancestors rejoice!

Forged for Wholeness: A Lovers Soul Invocation

I don't want a relationship.
I want a soul match.
A soul companion, in human form, here on Earth.
A reuniting with the one
who has danced beside me
in lifetimes before.
Who knows the shape of my laugh
the scent of my joy
the terrain of my wounds.
I want a *playmate of the gods.*
Someone I can drift into dreamy moments beside
curled on the couch mid-conversation
as a half-watched movie flickers across our relaxed faces.
A velvet-souled wanderer
who lays next to me on the floor
halfway through unpacking groceries
caught in a kiss that forgets time.
No performance. Just peace.
Someone I can laugh with
until we tumble into that rare kind of joy
that leaves us breathless, salt-teared
and utterly alive.
Someone who sings off-key
and still believes it's a beloved hymn.
Who calls my stretch marks *celestial maps*
and my quirks *divine blueprints.*
Who finds pleasure in the ordinary
pomegranate seeds shared one by one
mismatched socks worn boldly
our fingers laced like roots and constellations.
Someone with whom I build
not a perfect life
but a soul-rich one with.

A co-creation of meaning
rooted in everyday rituals;
side-by-side kitchen duties, and fluffing pillows, candlelight on a Tuesday
and memories of childhood
that come alive over shared meals and tender recollections.
I want to feast on life with them
cheeky, messy, sincere, and holy.
To create *love* as we weave celestial magic
and also like we're just
very, very famished.
Together we savour
the field of intimacy
where lovemaking
becomes a temple of touch
one to another
slow, delicious, and reverent.
Eye contact its own language
a blessed scripture.
passionate. . .ecstatic. . .blissful
A union of imagination
and creative bodies
receiving vessels
majestic landscapes
leading the way home.
Someone whose words I don't just hear
I *know* them
because our hearts speak fluent synchronicity.
Forged for wholeness.
I want the kind of connection
that echoes ancient myths
not to reenact the legend
but to live the truth beneath it.
A timeless creation story.
We'll bicker sometimes—
sure.
But we'll make up
with the *devotion* of star-crossed souls

who've finally landed
in the right realm.
We'll belly laugh until one of us snorts.
We'll cry, too
not only in pain
but in awe
when the world cracks open
to reveal another layer of *wonder.*
We'll hold hands in the grocery store
like two adolescents, giddy on avocados and hope.
We'll climb mountains
and dance in the rain.
We'll stay in bed all weekend
every moment equally sacred.
The one whose hand I hold
and feel the universe expand
a cosmic tether reminding us
that no storm, no sorrow, no season
can shake what we've cultivated.
And at night, when I close my eyes
they'll already be there
the one who visits my dreams
like a welcome guest
guiding us gently across the night sky
even as we sleep, curled close
our bodies breathing each other's peace.
No, I don't want a relationship.
I want a presence that feels like *sacred ground.*
Someone who sees my whole self
holds my contradictions tenderly
and tends to my soul
as if it were a garden blooming in real time.
And I will *offer* the same
to him
as well as the differences he desires.
So no,
I don't want a relationship.

I want the wild, wondrous *union*
of best friends turned cosmic allies
of sacred fools who know how to play and bow
and strip down to their essence.
I am open to *that.*
To the one who is my firelight
and my favourite soup.
My holy mischief
and my starlit calm.
Someone whose love isn't just safe
it's reverent and *true.*
Because I was never meant for the half-hearted.
I was forged
for wholeness.
partnership. . .union. . .love

The Womb of Change

The Womb of Change
is both cradle and catalyst.
She holds you when you fall apart.
She stirs you when you've lingered too long.
She is the breath before the leap,
and the fire that makes wings of your doubt.
She cradles what was,
midwives what is,
and calls forth what longs to be.
You do not enter her—you are her.
You are the tremble of first light,
the hush before emergence,
the pulse of possibility wrapped in skin.
The Womb of Change is both cradle and catalyst.
She is You.
So, rise not with haste,
but with holy knowing.

Touch your own skin
like sacred fertile soil,
and speak to your soul
like a beloved friend,
finally come home.
You are birthing the next true version of yourself.
You are enough. You are ready. You are beloved.
Now begin.

Raise the Stakes on Tenderness

A love letter to presence in long-term partnership,
with eyes open and heart unguarded.

Do not go to sleep.
The world may close its eyes,
but you—
you must stay awake.
Find your beloved in the quiet hush of ordinary moments.
See them.
Not as a name you know by rote,
but as the soft edges shifting in the candlelight
of each arising.
Comfort is not an excuse to vanish
while lying beside someone who would bleed for your joy.
To know someone
is not to fold them up into tidy conclusions.
We are all revision,
drafts rewritten in the ink of living.
Yes,
learn their values,
the anchor-points of their ocean. . .
commitment,
kindness,
loyalty,
love offered in gestures both grand and small.

Know their many languages of love,
spoken not always in words,
but in how they create a home around you
or hold your gaze when you falter.
Be the one who meets them anew each day,
with wonder,
with intention.
Who offers without hesitation,
who gives without erosion,
who makes of presence
a safe sanctuary.
Raise the stakes
on your own tenderness.
Match effort with vulnerability,
match words with the poetry of action.
Be the partner
who does not drift off into assumption,
who does not nap through another's ache,
who keeps the lamp of connection lit
even when the room is dim with routine.
Stay awake—
stay aware.
Even in silence,
reach for their hand
like it is still your first time.
Do not go to sleep
on the one
you promised
to love awake.

Dear Reader, now it's your turn to write. Use the blank space below. Try not to censor yourself.

There's something **BIGGER** stirring now!

Allow your words to rise from that stirring within; those deep inner promptings. Perhaps they come from a younger, softer part of you seeking attention, or from a higher wisdom-keeper truth part. What desires to expand bigger?

Lulu Pearl Trevena is a multi-award-winning author, Soulful Living Coach, retreat leader, and Creatrix of *Live Life with Wonder.* She supports women, especially in midlife and beyond, to reclaim their voice, pleasure, and feminine power through embodiment practices and soulful living. Her sacred offerings include the Silver Nautilus award-winning book *Soul Blessings, Moments of Transformation* card deck, and *Epiphany Journal & Playbook.* Lulu is the visionary behind *Wholehearted Wonder Women 50 Plus,* an international bestseller and global community.

A poet, truth whisperer, and wonder-seeker, she invites women to gently shed outdated narratives and awaken their inner radiance. She is changing the societal narrative about women and age. Her healing anthem, "Tender, Tender, Beloved," echoes her own transformation (available on her website).

She lives near the ocean and believes we're never too "grown-up" for wonder, nor too late to begin.

Explore Lulu's sanctuary on Substack *(Pearl Lustre with Lulu).*

Connect with Lulu: https://livelifewithwonder.com/

Chapter 13

Reluctance

...With Reasons to Go

Marquis "13 of nazareth" Mix

My Story

What you're about to read exists because I'm currently reluctant to write and share about healing. So much so, I told Laura. Why, you ask? Well, for the past seven years, I've been dealing with issues regarding my mental health; not a new experience, but the most difficult I have endured. So difficult, in fact, that I'm unwilling to share it here (not yet healed). However, I'm willing to share the following.

I've lived with epilepsy and seizures my entire adult life. The first one happened in October of 1994. It was almost unexpected. It was traced to a head injury I suffered during a car accident in April of the same year. Rather than get into the story here, I encourage you to listen to a rap song I recorded entitled "Head Trauma" which details the process. Nod your head to it by visiting the link below. https://13ofnazareth.bandcamp.com/album/fallout-shelter-an-epileptics-epic?t=4

After the diagnosis, I sank into depression. My family watched me closely with a deep sense of concern. I was uncomfortable. I was afraid. I stayed home more often. I ate my pain. I was also a high school senior and gained over 60 pounds before the end of the school year. Yeah, that part.

I spent roughly two years not caring about outcomes and bouncing from experience to experience. I had a treasure trove of life, but it was not the best life I could've been living.

I finally, due in part to the death of my favorite rapper, Tupac Shakur, on my 20th birthday, and in part due to an unexpected awakening, snapped out of depression and got back to life. It was indescribable.

To go back further, my mother and my maternal grandmother both died in 1990. Under the weight of tragedy and trauma, I became a thirteen-year-old adult that year. I don't believe I've healed. I think of them often; sometimes I cry.

I could catalog a litany of things, but the above is enough to make my points. Healing shows up in a variety of ways and some take longer than others. Healing can be unexpected or a result of diligent work. When healing hasn't shown up, it's not necessarily, but can be, the result of a reluctance to. . .

1. open up.

2. let go.

3. un-shoulder responsibility for things you cannot/could not change.

In the healing process, it's completely okay to be reluctant, but challenge yourself to move anyway. Move with pain. Move with fear. Move with doubt. It might take years, but the treasure trove of experience gained in the meantime will be worth it. And if you cannot make it all the way to healing during your lifetime, at least strive to make great memories along the way, and maybe, just maybe, even write about it. You just might be someone's unexpected motivation to get back to life, whole. Reluctant with reasons to go.

The Poems

love affair

misery will love you
until beauty becomes grotesque
and silence becomes painful

misery will leave you
wearing its fragrance
as a reminder to self
and sign to the world

misery is intimate
and disrespectful
it breaks up with you
by breaking you up inside
and trying to heal
tends to produce more

misery will teach you
patience by stitching
your mouth and heart closed

until one day
trying to heal
does not produce
more misery
and that's love
or at least
it feels like love
after being
in relationship
with misery

pass tense

i was
afraid to move
forward

i was
reasons I could not
explain

i was
uncomfortable width
the weigh

i was
gaining confusion
daily

i was
ounces of increase
unseen

i was
adding pounds
until

i was
unrecognizable shape
one year

i was
later in the journey too
myself

i was
a closed casket
walking

i was
round in circles
dying

i was
changing colors
darkness

i was
afraid to move
forward

i was
a series of decisions
to go

i was
any way
i could

i was
trying
to prove

i was
here

shaken not scared

I am a trip to the hospital waiting to happen
I am the shattering of my loved one's nerves
I am consciousness with temporary amnesia
I am flying down a flight of stairs face first

I am conversation without recall
I am biting my tongue until it bleeds
I am the lost control of motor skills
I am piss in a new pair of jeans

I am chaos without warning
I am the alteration of previous plans
I am laying helpless in a crosswalk
I am the reason for unusual traffic jams

I am dependent upon the kindness of strangers
I am falling at your feet all the time
I am a soft heart trapped in a hard place
I am vulnerability personified

I am always struggling to figure out why
I am here in the last place I ever dreamed
I am staring death in the absence of a face
I am a crumbling bridge over a troubled stream

I am crashing into the fire hydrant at the corner
I am limp body against airbag and car door
I am crashing into the walls of crowded venues
I am limp body against a hotel lobby floor

I am oxygen mask and intravenous fluids
I am fractured bones and sutured flesh
I am sharp pains and missing time
I am involuntary movements and dripping sweat

I am an earthquake with self-awareness
I am a tornado with arms and legs
I am twenty years living with epilepsy
I am shaking but I am not scared

stability in motion

when Taalam said, ". . .this, the most spiritual art."
what i heard was
spokenword is the art of getting to God for living
but to make living getting to know life
is a dangerously small circle with the deadliest price
for no one who loves you initially wants to believe
that you would nothing with your talent and/or degrees
other than stand before crowds and speak
in rhythms performing exorcisms with lyricism
because there ain't no money in the salvation business of self and kind
especially when the salvation rhymes
holding mirrors up to the eyes of anyone looking in its direction
plus, prophets don't get to profit off their own lives
and usually aren't considered prophets until they die
for the very reason they tried to explain they were alive
but once the caskets close and the urns are disposed of
the conspirators gather round to show the prophets love
because the profits in reminiscing
over what was once considered
to be the bane of one's existence
remember Jesus was slain by members of his own religion
Christianity was not existent
though parts of its evolution give his life, but one dimension
I hear he was totally dive and totally human
preaching the gospel in casual conversation with prostitutes
transmuting water into wine; I'm sure he drank some too
because in Hebrew celebrations that what sometimes do
doesn't make him any less divine
does make him more approachable
because the way in the almighty is usually portrayed
getting closer to the Most High puts most right feet in the grave
but a soul Jesus' stature was so alive and so brave
that the beaches where you wanna go on vacation
he would go just walk on the waves
but the people claiming to have the most faith nowadays

be living the most afraid
how you believe in God scared
of creations that live in submission to divine will
how you in God scared
when dominion over creation was one of the first divine gifts
and God said, "you can have whatever you like" way before T.I. did
but I understand, when dealing with the word
it's all about letter placement
see I realized when I was writing these lines
the same letter used to spell scared can be rearranged to spell sacred
and in this matrix, you are one or the other, but you can't be both
well technically you could but it wouldn't be conducive to growth
and no, faith does not mean life presents itself as you hope
faith means however life presents itself you will be able to cope
with a smile on your soul like don't I make this look easy
don't my stare look like it's healing
don't my laughter remind you of children
don't my posture look like I'm always chillin'
we be going through the same shit, but don't I always look different
that's just the result of getting to life for a living
the outside is difficult still
the inside however is just still
for stability with the motions of life is God's will
stability within the motions of life is God's will
stability within the motions of peace be still
peace be still
peace be still
but even if it's not
I will still be peace

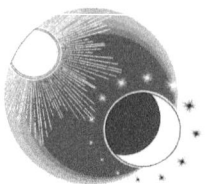

Dear Reader, now it's your turn to write. Use the blank space below. Try not to censor yourself.

Have you ever been so frustrated with the course of life that you constantly give yourself ways out of moving? If you are willing to challenge your reluctance with any reason; a single step forward is possible.

Marquis "13 of nazareth" Mix is a poet and spokenword recording artist from Virginia, living with epilepsy, a dry sense of humor, and striving for peace of mind over everything. Over the course of a twenty plus career, Marquis has toured throughout the United States, Canada and the United Kingdom appearing at venues including but not limited to over 50 colleges and universities, The Julliard School, The Carter Baron, The New Jersey Performing Arts Center and The Saint Lawrence Center For The Arts, published eight spokenword albums and featured on the Grammy nominated album *"Civil Writes: The South Got Something To Say."*

Connect with Marquis: https://13ofnazareth.net

Chapter 14

A Journey of Love
An Opening After a Twist in Destiny
Donna O'Toole, R.N., B.Ed., Reiki Master, End of Life Doula

My Story

Have you ever heard whispers that don't come from the lips of someone else, but somewhere deeper, between the worlds of the seen and the unseen, the known and the unknown? Sometimes they appear in the quietude just before dawn, or in the stillness of heartbreak. I hear whispers, but not with my ears.

It's not easy for me to write on demand. *Why can't I write like others? Words just seem to flow from their pen. They write such flowery descriptions.* I look down at the sheet of paper and see I wrote three words: *See Spot run.* Not really, but that is what it feels like to me.

Until. . .

I listened from the space of the ache within my heart, with the tears that knew what my voice couldn't say. One day, I let those emotions move into my heart space. I tasted, smelled, touched, heard, and felt those raw feelings as words. Each tear became a word dripping across the stained paper. Authoring poems became my way of touching my inner world of emotions that I couldn't or didn't want to express aloud.

Sometimes, a poem finds me before I even know it's something I need to hear.

I no longer feel alone as something beyond me begins to speak. I feel something shift, like a gentle pull tugging at the edge of my awareness. A sacred nudge saying, "Pay attention."

And I can do nothing else but listen—with my heart.

That's when I know I'm being guided.

Rev. Nancy Mercurio, Unity of Tampa's minister, talks about God's positioning system. I liken it to a GPS for my soul. To me, it doesn't speak in maps or directions but in feelings, signs, and symbols. This is a guidance system, divinely timed, designed to show me a direction I need to go in.

And it's in these precise moments that poetry begins to rise. I cannot do anything else but write. Actually, I don't write; it writes for me, somehow shaping what I already know. I become a translator of words moving through me.

And while the poem may come to offer something to others, it always first heals something in me. Shifts me. Transforms me.

It's how I remember who I am.

These poems are part of my inner GPS: God's way of recalibrating me when I detour off course, reminding me of the deeper journey I'm here to take. They guide me not to a destination, but to an alignment—with my spirit, my soul's purpose, my truth, and my authenticity.

So, I listen.

I write.

I find my way home again.

This is the *Journey of My Heart*—a journey with a twist in destiny I never saw coming. Through the act of writing, I found healing and grace. And somewhere along the way, my heart opened in ways I didn't know were possible.

When I'm quiet enough. . .

. . .my soul whispers back.

The Poems

My Beloved, My Love

My Beloved,
In you, I have found
A friendship deeper than
The winding roots of sturdy trees,
A love more magnificent than
The wild open skies.

My Beloved One,
Your voice is the song
I want to hear
Each morning when I wake
And each night as I fall asleep.

You are the first voice I seek
When the world shifts around me,
You are the earth beneath my feet,
Steady, strong and unmoving,
Your loving presence
Turns my chaos to calm.

In your presence,
Time slows, not stopping,
Allowing us to live
Only in the present moment.

Your caress
Is a loving declaration
Carved softly
Upon my soul.

Your touch is not a flame,
But a tender warmth
Left behind,
Lingering ever so
Lightly on my skin

Long after the fire
Of your touch fades.

I do not love you
Because the sun rises,
The moon glows,
Or the stars glimmer.
I love you for the spaces
In between
Where light dances
Among the gathering shadows,
Where all becomes still
And your presence remains.

My Beloved,
Our love is a quiet current
Beneath the surface,
Pulling us closer and deeper.
Its strength is unspoken
But quite undeniable.

Our love is not made
Of grand gestures,
But of moments—
A glance across a crowded room;
Your hand brushing mine
Without thought;
The smile that lights your face,
The twinkle of your eyes
When you look at me,
The weight of your silence
That feels fuller and richer
Than any words could convey.

We love and carry each other
Without asking,
Without measuring
Who gives more,
Because there is no ledger in this.
Only the knowing in our hearts,
You are mine, as I am yours,
Not in ownership, or possession,
But in trust, love and grace.

Our love does not clamor
For the world to see it,
It lives in the stillness
Of shared mornings,
The laughter that rises
Like sunlight breaking
Through rainclouds,
The gentle kisses that
Leaves dew upon our lips.

My Beloved,
This love is ours—
Unfolding in ways
No one else will ever touch,
A love that breathes like the sea,
A friendship that anchors us
Even as waves rise and fall.

In your laughter,
I find a mirror of my own joy.
In your silence,
I hear the unspoken truths that bind us.

We are not just lovers—
We are companions on a path
Worn soft by shared steps,
By dreams that overlap
Weaving our life together.

I treasure the way my hand fits in yours,
Not as a completing puzzle piece,
But as a promise—
That in all my pieces,
You only see me whole.
With you, love is not a demand
Or a performance.
It is a kindness joined
With compassion and honesty;
A light that never grows dim
But neither blinds or burns.
Your love is a gift,
Providing a soft safe place to rest,
Cradled within your tender embrace.

Let time unravel
Weaving its intricate tapestry.
Let the years inscribe
Their stories upon our hearts.

But you,
My Beloved,
My Love,
Will always be
The keeper of love's
Sweetest song to embrace.

A Twist in Destiny

You came strolling into the restaurant
Suitcase in tow
Choosing the table diagonal from me
You selected the seat
Facing my direction.

I surprised myself
When I boldly asked
"Are you coming or are you going?"

Your gentle, calm voice
With a hint of laughter
Replied "Coming, and You?"

And in that instance
I knew there was
A familiarity in your voice,
A knowing,
A connection.

It was our souls
Recognizing each other
Through our mutual and
Interconnected vibrational frequency.

The familiarity that does not come
From this lifetime
But from somewhere much older
As if the stars once shined light
Of this meeting to happen
In this lifetime.

Did we have a karmic understanding
To seal some unfinished business
To taste our love for
One more brief shining moment
In this lifetime?

I believe the way
Unique synchronicity events
Conspired for Us to meet
Meant We were destined
To be together.

I thought I understood
How destiny worked.
Each of Us placed
In a space and time
Guided by the divine hand
That sees everything.

I felt the universe
Carve your name
Into the fate lines
Of my hand and heart.

I felt the divine hand
Guiding our path
Until we found
Our hearts afire with love.

But sometimes God's divine plan
Unravels in unexpected ways
From what we thought
Was meant to be forever.

I waited for some miracle
To happen
I waited for some sign
To say this was not the end.

However,
I felt the silence of your touch,
Your name that lingered
Upon my lips,
The hand which no longer
Reached out to mine.

I stand on this side of ending,
Knowing that just sometimes
Stars are meant to burn
And not meant to hold.

Concluding sometimes
Love is not about holding onto someone,
As that would destroy
The beauty of what We had.

Knowing sometimes
It is not about forever, but
Love is about letting go.

Understanding,
Our time and
Our love
Was written in
And part of the
Master design all along.

I will always carry
You in my heart
Because our love
Was not a regret.

I no longer ask
Why Us ended,
But look at the gifts
Of our journey,
Finding even detours
Can be divine.

Softly go My Beloved,
As my departing gift to you,
Know
Our love lived
Our love shined brightly
Our love marked
A time that called to Us.

Finding Clarity with an Abyss Between My Heart and My Mind

There is this standoff
Between my mind
And my heart.
I feel as if
My heart is held hostage
By me not letting you go
As my mind keeps
Negotiating the terms.

My heart aches
With the pain of losing you, and
My mind has memorized
Every reason I
Should stop loving you
And move on.

But my heart only
Remembers the love we shared,
The sound of your voice,
The way your head tilted
When you laughed,
The shine and twinkle of your eyes
When you looked at me,
The way you always
Reached for my hand
And opened your arms
To hold me close
In the sweetest of embraces,
Our deep conversations
About life, death
And living our dreams.

Each step I take now
Feels like a betrayal

Of my love for you.
And just maybe I will
Understand that the
Answer is not in the choosing,
But holding both truths
Of my mind and my heart.

That I loved you so deeply
With my every breath and all my heart,
The vice gripping and clenching pain
Reminds me daily,
I miss you and our friendship dearly.
But I deserve more,
I deserve peace of mind,
And I choose peace in my heart.

One day my mind
Will default to my heart.
When the mind accepts
What the heart sings.
I know I am love and
My heart knows the love
Is always there.

I will fill the abyss as
I come to understand
That letting you go
Does not mean that
I stop loving you,
But that I can in time
 Find the place where
I am holding both truths,
Resolving the disconnect and

Being congruent with my mind
And my heart,
Knowing I deserve peace.
I deserve more
Than you could give.

The lightbulb is turned on
Realizing,
It is not in just any one moment,
But an accumulation of many things,
When clarity seems to
Come out of nowhere,
Appearing suddenly and
Unexpectedly welcomed.

Understanding that
Love is not enough
When it has nowhere to go.

I believe that even upon my final hour,
My slowing earthly breaths,
My fragile beating heart will
Still be full of my
Undying love for you.

Even my last breath of love
Will carve your name
Upon my heart.

And in reflection I understand
There were no fanfares,
No warnings,
But in the presence of
Only one heartbeat
I am aware
I can breathe easily
As I emerge from
My cocoon,
Freeing myself from the
Bondages of my past.

I am the butterfly,
and
I set myself free,
Shedding old patterns and
Embracing new beginnings.

Flapping my wings,
Getting my bearings
I yearn for flight.

I let go.
I let it go.
I let you go.

I am choosing
To rebirth myself
On my new journey.
Joyfully loving each and every day,
Listening to my voice within,
Awakening fresh ideas and
Rising to breathtaking heights.

I am free to fly
In any direction.
Wondering where the winds
Will entice me
To adventure today.

I reach to the heavens
Transversing the currents
Bravely soaring to unknown places,
Being authentic and
Becoming everything
I was meant to be.

Come soar with me.
Fly in Freedom,
Fly in joy, love and light,
Fly with abandonment.

I am the butterfly,
Free to be Me.

The Illusion of Us

What is love?
Is it the emotion or feeling
Shared between us?
Or is it. . .
I love the me
I become
Loving you?

Last September you said
Those three magical words to me
I Love You!
They entered my heart
And coursed through my veins
Reaching every cell
In my body, mind and heart.

Those words imprinted
Their image on the journey
Of how I perceived you
And how I perceived us.
Is our love real?
Or did I create an
Enchanting illusion?

I shared my whole heart
To you willingly
Without thinking what
I would gain in return.
Through our time together
I built a love story
Around every image
I saw in the mirror
Until those reflections
Became the story
I wanted to see and believe.

Did I not see the red flags
Because I had put on
My rose tinted glasses?
Did I become so blind
I could not see the crack
In our mirror.

The red flag signs were there all along,
But was I holding a version of you
That I only wanted to see.
Did this version really exist
On this Earth plane?

So I ask,
What is the truth?
Is it the image or shadow
That stares back at me?
Or is it. . .
I love the me
I am still learning to see?

This September I heard
Three silent words from within—
I Forgive You.
And then surprisingly,
And more importantly,
I heard three more silent words from
within -
I Forgive Me.
These six words
Pulse through my beating heart,
Not to heal us,
But to free the parts of me
That still wanted you,
That still waited for you.

Cherished memories etched
Their shape and sound into my mind,
Not as the story we lived,
But as the story I had painted.
So, I ask
Is this healing real?
Or am I creating
A softer and kinder illusion?

I hold my whole self
To the light cautiously,
Knowing now the cost
Of giving without guard,

Of being in a relationship
Without setting healthy boundaries.

Reflecting during my time alone
I have dismantled our story
Until the mirror reflects back
What it wants me to see,
And its truth is no longer
What I want to believe—
It is simply what is.

But I took off my
Rose tinted glasses
And I see you as you really are
Knowing there never was an Us.
As Us was just
An Illusion of Me
Loving the Me
I became

Loving You.

Dear Reader, now it's your turn to write. Use the blank space below. Try not to censor yourself

When my soul whispers back to me, I hear _____.

Donna O'Toole, RN, B.Ed., Intuitive, Energy Healer, End of Life Doula.

After caring for her husband of 14 years, who died from ALS, Donna knew something was missing from Western teachings. As a result, she studied and merged the Western and Eastern philosophies to enhance her healing abilities.

Donna is also a Reiki Master, Karuna Reiki Master, crystal, sound, and color Healer. She is in her third decade of embracing the healing arts and energy work.

Donna's expertise focuses, as she feels called, on those individuals who need help with alternative healing options; transitioning from this earth plane; and those who have had the trauma of childhood sexual abuse.

Donna truly believes it's important to live your authentic spiritual life and be guided to be and dwell where it *makes your soul sing*.

Connect with Donna: sharingjoys@gmail.com

Chapter 15

Endless Dots. . .
Create New Perceptions and Possibilities

Rev. Dr. Karen Schuder, EdD, MDiv, MAM

My Story

I couldn't find the thoughts or words to begin a new life chapter. Silence within battled the noisy world outside. Rain struck the windows as dark clouds shifted. My gaze wandered from the blank computer screen to the raging storm outside, and a tear rolled down my cheek.

I was immersed in an empty house devoid of children's shouts and quick footsteps. No musical notes trilling through the rooms, nor requests for homemade cookies. Three beloved, grown children now live on their own.

My husband, Steve, and I did our job. It seemed like just yesterday when I wished I could get a few minutes alone. Our youngest child moved out years ago, but moments of longing still creep up on me.

Can I please go back in time?

This story's moment occurred when I was caught between trying to heal and start anew, from pastor to writer. The last congregation said, "We want you to help us change." A litany of complaints, financial deficits, and secret meetings revealed the insincerity behind these words. I handed in my resignation and walked out the door with a barrage of thoughts swirling through my mind.

No more getting chewed up by people who are supposed to be kind.
Does this mean I'm a failure?
No more trying to convince people to act on what they say.
Enough tears and banging my head against the wall.
I feel empty. Broken.

Months later, I sat at my desk trying to write a new start. Some days shyly held out new possibilities, but others were dark and rainy. On gloomy days, I especially missed the sounds of our children. I was envious of Steve, whose successful career still drew him out of the house.

The storm brewing outside released inner turmoil. Loneliness filled the house, and negativity flooded my thoughts. Like a child whose face pressed up against a foggy window, I struggled to see new possibilities.

Soft sounds of my dog licking her paw broke through the mental barrage. I turned to see Karma's brown, soulful eyes looking at me. As a retired sled dog, she modeled resilient change. When we first welcomed her into our lives, she stared at the steps going into our house, not knowing what they were or where they'd lead. Now she was settled into a different life.

I moved from my desk and sat next to Karma curled up on the couch. I felt her slow, steady heartbeat as she rested her chin on my lap. My heart smiled. Our lives had changed and would continue to do so, yet hope was still there.

My phone's ringtone pierced the moment.

"Hello?"

"Hi Mom. . ."

Dear reader, I know how hard it can be to deal with change, challenge, and loss. May my poems inspire you to see healing possibilities and new, hopeful ways of understanding yourself. We are so much more than what one sentence can describe. Yes, we can create new stories.

The Poems

Endless Dots

Decades move on with life closely defined
Constrained with a period by "I am."
One sentence for a crowded life
But who can use a single dot?

With a world so full of circles that wind
Beyond this endless space of time
Move on and on past here and now
To push forward a brand-new plot

Another dot is added past the line
Opens wide more windows and doors
Giving rise to unexpected floors
Adding hope beyond one lone spot

Each step, each breath to somehow finally find
A reason to offer far more
To the I am who walks my shoes
Yet sight strains to see past a small jot

Can it be if I'm truly genuine
That this very full life of mine
Should really be seen as defined
By rows and rows of endless dots. . .

Bloom Dear Child Bloom

Bloom dear child bloom
Let your leaves reach afar.
Stems stand straight and tall while
Petals vibrate with brilliant colors.
Shine in your lush garden to radiate
Far beyond old fence posts.
Smile at the world as you
Sing out your name.

Bloom dear child bloom
No longer small nor pure.
I miss your youth yet while
Tears cloud my eyes I beam to see you shine.
My garden is full but also empty
As sunlight dims and shifts.
Colors often change yet
I will remain.

Bloom dear child bloom
Don't stop for me nor fear.
Let your roots grow deep while
Grasping joy and hope where sunlight sparkles.
My heart holds you everywhere and always
As time transforms our yards.
In a bigger bolder way
Bloom dear child bloom.

You Can't Change the Stripes on a Self-Proclaimed Leopard

Parched waving grass beckoned me towards a pool of tepid water.
Upon approach I saw a zebra kneeling behind a boulder.
With black and white stripes poking the sky, he observed nearby beasts.
It was odd to see so I asked, "Why are you staring so at these?"
"Can't you tell?" he said, "I am a hungry leopard hunting for game."
"But you're a plant-eating beast, one of the herd," I swiftly proclaimed.

"Nope. I'm a finely tuned predator as my many spots disclose."
I looked but not one lone dot was found among the black and white rows.
He motioned to the right and said, "My fearless leader told me so."
Beyond him I saw a quaking ostrich with its head in a hole.
The flightless bird raised its balding pate to give beady eyes a boost
Before croaking, "It's true. We ferocious leopards do rule the roost."

Shock held my tongue as I gazed upon the brazen, misguided pair.
They stared back at me with narrowed eyes as if challenging my dare.
I pointed to the prostrate equine blurting, "Can't you see your stripes?"
He shook his shaggy head and dust arose as his hooves took two swipes,
"You are sadly mistaken, don't convince me to see or be more."
My reply was stifled as a herd of zebras thundered to shore.

The curious zebra jumped and lunged towards the group with ears back.
Was he truly on a hunt for big game and going to attack?
He slowed to a saunter going forward with his shaggy head bowed,
As he entered the group his black and white stripes blended with the crowd.
I realized then, as hard as I might try, even with words tempered,
One cannot change or remove the stripes on a self-proclaimed leopard.

I paused, began to crouch, but then I duly questioned my outlook.
The tall grass waved me back to where I could see I'm an open book.
The audacious ostrich slowly crept off wearing a pouty frown.
My mind raced forward and questions emerged while I shyly looked down.
Were there black and white stripes or spots on display for all to see?
A smile curved my lips as I recalled exactly who I am to be.

I See You and I Care

Child with holes in faded red shoes
Staring towards nowhere
Holding hope on a spinning thread
I see you and I care

Woman with makeup-covered bruise
Trembling hands reach backwards
Longing for a different past
I see you and I care

Man with empty bottle of booze
Sitting on a corner
Staring at a raging war within
I see you and I care

Family with one suitcase to lose
Running towards a dim wall
Fleeing a bleak but cherished home
I see you and I care

Lover with bold rainbow tattoos
Clasping hands with rebels
Facing a world of foul judgment
I see you and I care

You with closed fists set to accuse
Trying to banish pain
Finding forgiveness a battle
I see you and I care

None of you need pay approval dues
Radiating inherent beauty
Bearing immeasurable value
I see you and I care

What can my heart and words refuse
Standing firm to proffer care
Moving past blinded crowds to show
I see you and I care

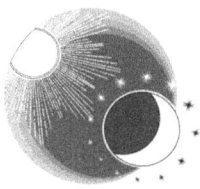

Dear Reader, now it's your turn to write. Use the blank space below. Try not to censor yourself

It's your turn to create new ways to see life and open doors of opportunity. Write down sentences describing yourself. Remove the periods and add new descriptions that inspire you to see more hope, joy, peace, meaning. . .

Karen Schuder, EdD, MDiv, MAM, speaker and best-selling author, has extensive experience promoting resilience and role sustainability. Years of helping people during traumatic times, leading organizations, and working globally inform her work with people in personal and professional helping roles. Karen offers life-changing concepts and practical strategies with an enjoyable, interactive approach. Check out her book *Resilient and Sustainable Caring: Your Guide to Thrive While Helping Others* and chapters in *100 Poems & Possibilities for Healing: Volume 2,* and *The Caregiver's Advocate: A Complete Guide to Support and Resources.* Learn more about how to promote resilience, increase healthy life balance, and decrease anxiety on her website.

Connect with Karen: http://www.karenschuder.com

Chapter 16

In the Moment

Moody Black

My Story

I used to hate to read! However, my mom was big on my sister and I reading poetry (i.e., Langston Hughes, Nikki Giovanni, Maya Angelou, et. al.). It wasn't until the age of eleven that I was bored and looked on my mom's bookshelf to find a book with cool pictures. I came across a book entitled *This Time Called Life* by Walter Rinder. There were these beautiful, soft black and white photos that caught my attention. Beside the photos were poems about being young and free. That inspired me to learn how to poetically express myself. After that, I grew to appreciate the poets my mom introduced to me. Around that time, I began to get into hip-hop. The rest, as they say, was history. Several albums later (both poetry and hip-hop), I wanted to create something special combining both art forms. I began with the intention of completing a full-length hip-hop project with 15-plus tracks, but as I looked back at the work I had already created, I realized the pieces I had were powerful on their own (poems and poetic raps). So, I decided to release nine tracks. Each verse and poem captures moments from different points in my life, reflecting my journey of growth, self-expression, and manifestation. While there are still tracks I didn't include here, they'll appear in my next—and possibly final—project. If you appreciate the lyrical storytelling of Outkast blended with the conscious wordplay of Common and De La Soul, this collection is for you.

The Poems

We Winning

Verse:

They criticize you from a distance
Feeling like you wanna lose religion
You didn't ask for those opinions
Hoping that folk just mind their business
But the grind continues, ya roll your sleeves
Tears fall and your nose leak
Cause you're trying to get where you 'pose to be
But the path is long, ya got swollen feet
They didn't see the times you were homeless
They don't understand your focus
The days you felt you were hopeless
That smile just meant you were coping
But plenty of times you could've folded with the pain you were holding
But you chose to win: so, keep going!!!

Speak it, we claim it, we uplifting. . .
The weight off our shoulders like we up lifting
We lost so much, look at us winning
We shining, now: they look at us different
We winning, we winning, look at us winning
We winning!
They only talk about ya when you're winning,
They only talk about ya when you're winning

Let's Get It!

Find Myself

Gonna find myself
Won't rewind myself
And I will ask for help
Won't deny myself
It's "Mr. Fish and Grits", "Mr. Downhome" With a lot
of hang-ups. . .I'm "Mr. Dial Tone," I'm your country
cousin, who can't get it right. . .As though it seems. . .so
hard for me to sleep at night So many loose screws, it's
hard to keep 'em tight So many dark days, it's hard to
see the light I made a lot of messes, I think I need a maid
I be cutting it close, my life can be fade. . .

Every day, I'm making my way
And though I will stray with every step
I'm finding myself and my spiritual wealth

I'm in this ocean of thoughts, I feel lost
I'm trying to get myself together at any cost
From my bad decisions, I paid a pretty penny
Went from "dime pieces" to not having any
I was broke as a joke: now, that's a famous quote
A Titanic metaphor, I was a sinking boat
Had my first child when I was sixteen
Thought I was ready for the challenge. . .Mitch Green
But there's a Mike Tyson punch for your big dreams
And they be waiting for your fall on the big screen
Divorced twice and I can't keep a girlfriend
I'm Captain Jack Sparrow sailing to "The World's End"
And that's on me, it's my fault
Had my hand in the cookie jar and got caught
But, I'm fine tuning for a different song
And if you been in my shoes: then, come and sing along

Every day, I'm making my way
And though I will stray with every step
I'm finding myself and my spiritual wealth

No Wings

We ain't got no wings, but we still want to fly
We ain't got no wings, but we still want to fly

Verse:

I want to dive into the velvet skies with closed eyes
But y'all can't conceive it with a closed mind
Cause y'all part of the machine. . .laundry mat
You're seeking change but ya really want the quarters back
Too much brainwashing. . .Got y'all on the clothes line
So quick to fold up when your soul dry
Sometimes i.wonder.what I'm made for
And I'm grindin hard enough for what I prayed for!
They say it's too late ya teeth getting longer
There's grays in your beard. . .the sun setting on ya uh
They feel I'm out of place like I'm Map Questin'
But ima show ya what I've learned. . .Call it Map Testin'
It's something over the clouds, I'm trying to see it
Show the milky way my "drip". . .I'm a speak it (spigot)
Manifest it for the blessings. . .then, I'ma leak it
They say the sky's the limit. . .then, I'ma reach it

We ain't got no wings, but we still want to fly
We ain't got no wings, but we still want to fly

Poem:

There's a cosmos out there
Waiting for me to sit on its front porch
Sippin' solar systems out of a Mason Jar
Waiting to consume the right moon shine to give me wings
Some say I'm delusional
But I'm gonna fly anyway
With an invisible wingspan that gets me to the south side of Saturn
And I'm hoping we all can get there
Cause there's a cathedral of constellations Waiting for our arrival
So, who's flying with me?

We ain't got no wings, but we still want to fly
We ain't got no wings, but we still want to fly

Fall In Love

Poem:

Your love is my libation
It's a liquid language that pours into me
It's meditation when my soul sips
The way your heart speaks to me
In other words, it's peace to me
Like listening to rain or watching a waterfall
And "falling" in love with you. . .is the greatest gift gravity ever gave me
And I want it forever!

Dear Reader, now it's your turn to write. Use the blank space below. Try not to censor yourself.

Pick an object that has witnessed your life (a shoe, mirror, pen, streetlight). Write a poem in its voice.

Moody Black has been captivating audiences as a performing artist since the age of twelve. Known for his dynamic stage presence and tireless work ethic, he has become a prominent figure on the multi-regional poetry scene. His impressive list of achievements includes:

TEDx Presenter

Winner of the 2015 National Poetry Awards Best Host of an Open Mic.

Awarded the 2019-20 Metropolitan Arts Council SmartArts Teaching Artist of the Year in Greenville, South Carolina.

Winner of the 2020-21 Upstate Music Awards Artist of the Year.

Named 2021 Southeastern Entertainment Awards Spoken-Word Artist of the Year.

Recipient of the 2022 Metropolitan Arts Council SEW-Eurodrive Minority Teaching Artist Fellowship.

Moody Black continues to inspire through his artistry, teaching, and commitment to uplifting others across various platforms.

Hi lb "I Th M " i il bl l i l

His new album "In The Moment" is available exclusively on Bandcamp.

Connect with Moody: http://www.moodyblack.bandcamp.com/

Chapter 17

How the Light Gets In

Fragments of Love, Loss, and Resurrection

Parushka Moodley

My Story

Poetry has never been homework for me. It has always been oxygen. As a child, I scribbled rhymes in the margins of notebooks, enchanted by the way words tumbled and skipped like marbles across a wooden floor. But the first time poetry stopped me in my tracks, it was Shakespeare who stole my heart. "Let me not to the marriage of true minds" was supposed to be just another sonnet, but it felt like a revelation. I felt my breath catch, the way it does when a lover grazes his thumb across your knuckles. The rhythm was steady, a secret heartbeat beneath the page. The words leaned toward me, as if they waited centuries just to arrive in me. That sonnet didn't just speak to me; it claimed me.

Like any great love, it wasn't always easy. It followed me into the darkest corners of my soul. I was drawn to poets who bled on the page—Sylvia Plath, Emily Dickinson, Virginia Woolf.

Their words were poison and antidote alike. I remember how sadness engulfed me under the blankets, tear-stained, my chest on fire with emotions I couldn't name. I devoured *Edge* and *Hope* in equal measure, grief and yearning tying knots like anchors.

By sixteen, I wrote my own, scrawling into notebooks with urgency, as though if I didn't release the words, they'd consume me whole. Messy, jagged, and violent sometimes—but they were mine. And they kept me alive.

Then came the shift when poems weren't just my confessions; they were a conversation, a bridge. What I wrote could mean one thing to me and something else entirely to someone else. It held multitudes, shapeshifting in another's hands. A line of love to me was someone else's heartache. And both would hold true.

That reciprocity, that's the miracle of poetry. It lives between us, waiting for us in the quiet, ready to become what we need most—a mirror, a hand to hold, a light in the dark.

Today, poetry is still my longest love story. It has carried me through grief, through silence, through every season of myself. It's how I speak to the girl I used to be, how I honour the people who saved me, and how I reach for the ones who need saving now.

And always, I return to the beginning, to Shakespeare's sonnet. "Love is not love which alters when it alteration finds." The line still flickers through me like a struck match. What it meant to me at sixteen is not what it means to me at forty, but that is poetry's gift, it never leaves, only deepens,

Because poetry, like love, does not waver. It carves itself into your bones, tracing the fractures, turning them into windows to let the light through. It has written itself into me, from the day I first held its hand and realised it would hold me for life.

The Poems

Here With Me

It's all blueprinted, organised, totally sane,
Dreams splashed like water on the embroidered duvet.
But as the tears fall recklessly, they echo through the haze,
And just for a second, I lose my way.

I scream, I cry, I tear at my flesh,
For reality's my hint, my cue to confess -
That I'm stuck, that I'm lost, that I don't know what to do,
That my dreams are illusions that will get me through.

Through the hurt, through the pain, through the cold, endless night,
Through the anguish and weight of a dying fight,
And the picture in my mind of the straight and narrow trail,
Begins to wind, begins to bend, and the rain turns to hail.

My eyes flutter open, and my world slips away,
Pinks and golds, facades that are grey.
And my life is warped into a single, honest plea:
All I've ever wanted is you, here with me.

The Drowning Hour

She sat still, deep in her reverie,
the world around her blurring.
      She sensed the laughter, the chatter.
She smelled the alcohol, the cigarette smoke.

But tears pressed at the edge of her sanity.
The pain all encompassing.
      It began in the pit of her belly,
but felt like the seat of her soul.
It burned.
It ate at her from the inside,
acid devouring delicate flesh.

It rose into her chest,
her heart pounding,
each beat sharper than the last.
It seeped into her veins,
a hot, burning liquid
that made her want to rip open her skin
so the agony might dissipate.

Every cell screamed for her to run.

Run and hide.
Run and jump.
Run and die.

But the sight of him
held her there,
paralysed in the palm of his hand
as he brushed her away
without a second thought.

She felt the splintering in her heart,
thin cracks like shards of glass
etching his name into
the core of her humanity.

A giggle.
A smile.
A hand on her shoulder.
She shuddered back into the room.
      Surrounded by people,
Yet utterly alone.

Their eyes met momentarily.
Nothing. Blank space,
hazel voids of emptiness.

She tipped her head back,
draining her glass,
drowning the pain
of being in love with him.

The House That Named Me Wrong

If you'd ever listened,
you'd know I love summer rain,
how it baptises my skin
with promises that the sun will return.

If you'd paid attention,
you'd know I love to write,
how the words spill from my fingertips,
ink unravelling truths
I'm not allowed to say out loud.

If you'd been watching,
you'd know I love art,
anything brave enough to bare its heart,
and expose the quiet ache inside it.

If you'd been around,
you would have known my love for animals,
souls untainted,
love without conditions,
     love I have yet to find in you.

If you'd heard me,
you'd know I root for the underdog,
the misfits, the marked, the outcasts.
They are my people,
because I know their kind of lonely.

If you'd understood,
you'd know I don't need shiny things.
Money never bought my love,
and it never bought our happiness either.

If you'd truly loved me,
you would have seen my thirst for truth,
not for painted fences,
nor smiling photos that lied,
and you would have loved me still.

But you never listened.
Never watched.
Never came.
Never stayed.
     Never heard.
Never tried.

So I will listen
to the melody of glass reassembling itself.
I will pay attention
to the pulse of the pain in my chest.

I will hear and understand
the cries of a little girl who learned to disappear.
I will be there for her.
I will stay.
I will show up for me.

It may take time,
but I will crawl from the wreckage.
I will grow the wings you clipped.
I will rise above the house that named me wrong.

And until then, as I heal,
I will lie in the ashes,
not as your child,
but as my own ghost,
    teaching myself,
        how to be reborn.

The Clearing

I think I loved him before I knew what love was.
A ghost of a feeling etched in my bones,
a pulse in the dark,
a whisper passed through centuries,
waiting for skin, for breath, for life.

Not love at first sight,
but something buried deeper,
like the rhythm of a name I haven't spoken
but always known,
the outline of a face
I could trace in the dark.
A song that played in another room for years,
each note curling heat into my veins.

The clearing in the middle of a forest,
air charged,
time slowing,
threads tangling,
and the breath between us saying,
"Oh, there you are."

He doesn't ask who I am.
He remembers.
The sound of my voice.
The scar on my knee.
The ways my eyes darken
when desire grows restless
Like he'd read the blueprint of me,
long before I arrived.

He says, "You're going to ruin me."
But it feels like a vow.
Something holy.
Something sacred.
Like ruin is just another word for returning.

His touch doesn't startle.
It recognises. It claims.
Hands moving across my skin like water,
Like worship,
like wonder.
A prayer learned by heart,
in a life he only half recalls.

We're not falling.
Just finding.
Surrendering.
Succumbing.
Two bodies pulled into the gravity of recognition.
Two halves of the same sentence,
complete at last.

I don't need to ask if he'll stay,
his presence is an answer,
ancient and unshaken.
His nearness humming through me,
His touch tangled into the heat of mine.

He sees every crack,
but chooses the light that leaks through.
He doesn't promise me forever.
He reminds me we've already had it.
We deepen like dusk,
the quiet thick with everything unsaid.

And when I open my eyes,
he's not beside me.
Only the hush of knowing,
the echo of something timeless,
spinning just out of reach.

I've dreamed him so deeply,
so completely,
so endlessly,
I think he's starting to dream me back.

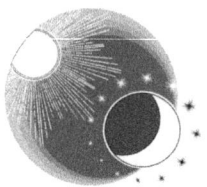

Dear Reader, now it's your turn to write. Use the blank space below. Try not to censor yourself.

If every chapter of your story stood before you, which page would you choose to turn to?

Parushka Moodley is a multi-hyphenate storyteller, screenwriter, and poet whose work blends sharp wit with unflinching honesty. She is the author of *The Everyday Girl's Guide to Douchebags,* a bold and relatable handbook that unpacks the messy world of modern dating with humour, candour, and just the right dose of rebellion. Her writing explores love, loss, self-discovery, and resilience, offering readers a voice that feels both intimate and universal. With a background in screenwriting, directing, and editing, Parushka brings a cinematic quality to her prose, weaving narratives that linger long after the page. Whether she is crafting poetry, fiction, or personal essays, her mission is to create work that inspires women to claim their power and embrace their stories unapologetically.

Connect with Parushka: https://instagram.com/iamparushka

Chapter 18

Anointed in Poetic Temples

'Neath Ever-Living Word Waterfalls

Sensei Timothy Stuetz

My Story

Nursery
Rhymes, my poetic start,
Yuck! Not that Humpty Dumpty again!

Mary had
A what? Itsy-bitsy
Spider—go thrill Jack and Jill—*baa, baa!*

Stories, toys
Cowboys, this young boy's joys.
Far from poetry I ride—for years.

Decades pass,
Fall in love, heart cracks.
Wow! There's poetry in me. Who knew?

Ink flows free,
Tracing love's lines, angles
And rhymes, till this chapter abruptly ends.

Burn poems!
Oh my, what have I done?
Love only sparked what's inside me!

Life crisis,
World construction crumbles.
In bed, I stay and cry for three days.

"God, if You
Exist, I must find You!"
Heart, soul, voice cry out—my core breakthrough.

God responds.
Signs I follow—some
Neon, some unseen—soul fire blazing.

Yoga, chants,
Taiji, meditation,
Reiki—heart bursts, poems flood forth.

CPA,
Left-brain train leaves station.
Dream chocolate *French Kisses* alive.

Brilliance blazes,
Create novel combo,
Poetry book hugs a teddy bear!

Poet Bear
Births. Love, visionary
Poems I pen after the *Burning*.

Peace, love, bliss,
I express ceaselessly—
Insights, truths, human injustices.

Bubble pops!
Mom says, **"Blew it, you did,**
Book should have been a children's story!"

"Nothing there,
For, about children, mom!
Not in my wheelhouse!" But my mom knew.

Out of blue,
Six months later, *Surprise!*
First children's story pops into mind!

Forty-four
Years later, still popping!
Two hundred ninety-two tales to date.

How? Why? Grace!
One hundred thirty-six
Beyond fabled Hans Christian Andersen.

Bliss Beary's
Fairy Tales Of The Heart.
Wisdom, love, and fun for all ages.

Rhymes and prose,
Original tale each,
Your imagination foundation.

Fairy Tales,
Creative genius sparks,
Fantasy and sensibility.

Einstein: "Want
Brilliant children? Tell them
Fairy tales." Well, proof's in the pudding!

And I'm the
Pudding! Forty years in,
Tales start flowing freely in rhyming.

I pen tales,
Ravenously read bio,
Spiritual, metaphysical books.

Pet pages—
Poems of Poet Saints.
Their books become Poetic Temples.

Poetic Temples
Where God's Grace anoints me.
Awakens my soul, empties my mind!

Rumi pyre,
Gibran insights, Hafiz,
Kabir, Tukaram, Namdev bhajans.

Sacred songs,
Rhythmic notes, fire 'n light,
Ancient voices echo between lines.

Divine words
Melt my heart, flood my eyes.
Yogananda, Mirabai, Lalla.

Wisdom pearls
Glistening in my eyes.
Irritants, now mother-of-pearl bright.

The Mother,
Baba Muktananda,
Chidvilasananda, Gurunath.

Words weaved
In Poetic Temples
Permeate, activate, consecrate!

Heal, inspire,
Stir sleeping souls awake.
Christ, Buddha, Krishna, Sai Baba too.

Amma, Sri
Auribindo—Pure peace,
Love, bliss, truth arrows pierce—anoint me!

Anoint you!
One great fire, many flames,
Let your flame flicker, dance, explode, write.

How? Why me?
At age seventy-three,
Tesla Tyme Poetry seeds secrets.

Tesla says,
Magnificence of Code
3:6:9, holds keys to Universe.

Turn, turn, turn,
Tesla Poetry key,
Unlock Universal mysteries.

Syllables,
Line one, 3; Line two, 6;
Line three, 9. Now, it's versify time.

Tesla Threes,
Harmonic harmonies,
Pen uniting mind, body, heart, soul.

Tesla Tiers,
Stack lines three, story grows.
Three, six, nine stanzas—ready-set-GO!

Choose your words,
Let them bloom—love notes, memes,
Affirmations, logos, ads, posts, books.

Potent force,
They design. Strong, they are.
Language they shape, children's minds they guide.

Older minds,
A poetic pep pill.
Tesla Tyme Poems—shift lives, shape worlds!

Poetic
Temple, you're reading in—
'Neath Ever-Living Word Waterfalls!

The Poems

May my sparks
Light your Kundalini,
Igniting your Creativity!

Never Ever Again!

The "I" I was at birth,
Quickly evaporated into the chaos and clouds of Earth.
 The me "I" became, I did not know,
 As the pain of being me slowly did grow.

Pain eventually exploding like a fateful match struck,
Igniting a silent scream, louder than a roaring hot rod.
 I must find the One to whom I pray at night—God,
 Now lost somewhere amidst the daily muck.

A silent scream, rocket flames from a soul yearning to *Remember.*
Remember even a trace of the "I" I was. Even a smoldering ember,
 Amidst this seemingly bottomless pit, this dark night of the soul,
 Teeming with despair, as if sucked into an inescapable black hole.

I didn't know my silent, piercing scream spawned a lightning rod,
Shooting up through Earth's chaos and clouds, this dark night of the soul,
 To reunite me with the "I" I was, the I AM that is God.
 The "I" I AM, that for decades, through chaos and clouds clawed.

The "I" that I AM now sees all life shimmering in and as Light,
With soft eyes shining bright,
Ears attuned to an inner divine thunder,
A once restless mind, empty of all but peace and insight,
A heart brimming with bliss, love, and wonder!

The "I" I was at birth, I did *Rediscover!*

I'm a *trip,*
You're a *trip,* why'd we take
This *Earthly trip?* Why'd we leave true hOMe?

Many *trips,*
Different paths to one end,
From mind to body, each step tells tales.

Mystery
Trip itinerary,
Not even day planner, country known.

Soul does know,
Mind not so. Family,
Life qualities—A *trippy* surprise.

Rush, we *trip,*
Mind lost in future's grasp,
Feet tangle, bumble, stumble, hit hard.

Brave we BE,
Setting sail on such *trip,*
True teachers few, tricksters that *trip,* many.

Mind trip zone,
Reality blurs fast,
Perception twists, heart truths slip through cracks.

Kicks we sought,
Kicks in asses we got,
A few sweet kisses too, way too few!

Power trip,
Some rule with a false hand,
Strength in control becomes control's trap.

Guilt trip placed,
Weights, heavy on the heart,
Let intentions shine through kindness.

Don't *trip* out,
Mind spins—what may come in?
Re-al-i-ty warps, con-fused, drift afar.

Pleasures' price,
Exacts its toll, sometimes
Now, sometimes down the line, no escape!

Trip words fast,
Tongue tangles, mind swirls too,
Lost in language, meaning breaks apart.

Don't you *trip*,
Over worry or fear!
Life flows best when we let go and flow.

Follow heart,
Do learn, love with each breath,
Blessed to find true *Guru Trip Guide*.

Round trip chit,
Thankfully we were given,
Timeless hOMe, here we cOMe, what a *trip!*

Memory,
A nostalgic pathway,
Trips down lanes where time feels still yet gone.

I'm a *trip*,
You're a *trip, Earthly trip*
Took to learn: **Never Ever Again!**

Ignorance Is Not Bliss!

They taught me . . .
to read, write, do arithmetic, cook, drive a car, earn a living.

They didn't teach me . . .
about relationships, setbacks, arguments, illness, pain.

How to handle children, bills, deadlines, foreclosures, traffic, divorces.

About my mind's superpowers and traps.

I was responsible for my own happiness.

There's more to life than my five senses detect and life's circumstances.

Concepts and beliefs are just that—
concepts and beliefs!

I did learn . . .
it wasn't safe to express myself.

Being a "good boy" was the only way to "get by—survive."

Not to trust—first others, then myself.

To criticize!

They didn't tell me . . .
I could see everything—*Everything*—superimposed
on a silken screen of crystalline light.

Such vision
would become my "normal" way of seeing.

I could find a stillness beyond silence—hear the "sounds of silence"—
within my own being.

It was possible to experience
such stillness smack dab amid daily activities.

I could always relate to the world with the wonder of a child—
seeing a freshness, newness in all people, plants, animals, events.

I could feel the Universal Energy supporting ALL life constantly
pulsating in my body—bathing every cell in a
delectable, indescribable golden warmth.

They didn't teach me . . .
about Love. Life. How to Live.

How to experience all of life as part of Me!

To see the exquisite beauty of every person.

Oh, my friends . . .
life is such a *thrilling* experience when we wake up!

With each step we take in understanding and living
as our true essence—*Love*—we come closer
to what is termed *Enlightenment.*

Enlightenment—our natural beingness embodied.

Our enlightened, electrified body is designed for
transmitting our heart's golden radiance
out to every cell, through every pore.

Out to every person, plant, and animal we greet.

Experiencing the flow of love within, as one might imagine
a "live" wire experiences the flow of electricity.

Enlightenment's
an ever-expanding experience of our own
Heart Flame,
Perfection!

Our own
God Self Radiance!

Yin-Yang-One, I AM

God, I have run sometimes fast, sometimes slow,
through all variations of your Creation:

The contrasting circus of New York City—
from the majestic business district to the garbage-
heaped alleys to the greenness concentrated in Central Park.

The eerie docks and musky lakefront of Chicago to a
wilderness preserve on its periphery where tall, old trees dim the
light above, as my feet softly crush layers of fallen leaves.

The awesome splendor of D.C.,
with its monuments graciously revealing wonders
of man and Self, while simultaneously housing those who wage war.

Florida's back country, amongst
tall pines, swamps, bees, snakes, and alligators—
lost in the artful dance of a butterfly floating above.

Atlanta's inner city,
constantly glancing about in fear,
to its outskirts, where rolling hills and thick pines
shelter my fears as the rising sun's morning ray's filter
through multicolored leaves on a statuesque old tree.

Dallas's barren flats,
with only the concrete and glass erections
of a fast-paced society breaking my eyes' line of sight.

Salt Lake City's serene nature trails,
bundled against the freezing chill of winter, ice hanging from
my moustache, marveling at snow-flaked flora as my feet lay tracks
next to a bunny's. Branches, diamond-studded, pressed from the evening freeze,
reflecting the sun's rays in colorful prisms splashed
against dawn's bright, baby-blue skies.

The barren splendor
of Arizona's deserts, the sun's
intense heat pulling raindrops of sweat out
through the wide-open pores of my sweltering body.

The old town structures
of New Orleans' French Quarter, as a myriad of
manifestations of the One Inner Self pass before my eyes.

The hustling cities of
Las Vegas and Reno, aglitter with
lights bright enough to tan my skin and
eyes searching for an everlasting high or big payday.

The crisp, pine-scented air of Tahoe,
where sapphire blue waters peek out from behind tall
redwood stands, dwarfed by snow-capped peaks cradling the lake.

The aloha of Hawaii,
where faces of the world gaze upon
palm-lined beaches; barren lands of volcanic ash;
billowy clouds suspended in heavenly blue skies; rainbow-filled valleys;
and high-rise buildings hiding tin shacks of an ancient, yet recent, past.

Washington state,
where clouds, sky, trees,
ferns, flowers, berries, mountains,
oceans, lakes, fresh air, and butterflies
unite in a magnificent blend of nature's graciousness.

Some runs brought inner peace
solely from the beauty of the outer setting, while
others were encased in fear, also arising from the outer setting.

The cliff paths of Huntington Beach,
sweating profusely at times, enthralled by the graceful
swoops of pelicans and gulls, the thunder of waves, and
the beauty in piers, people, and popsicles,
where, at the time Baba left his body:

To the left . . .
A full moon rises ominously slow and huge,
cooling the traffic that rushes by.

To the right . . .
A soft orange sun sets swiftly.
First, as a large beach ball balancing on the ocean.
Then as a dome containing the warmth of an Indian Summer.
Finally, as a disappearing dot, leaving its glow of reds, yellows, and oranges
on the horizon, cooled by the endless rush of the surf.

The simultaneous full moon and sunset,
night shadows and light,
the crashing waves.

And . . .

I'm in a tunnel, running faster than ever,
between these two seemingly contrasting worlds.

At the end of the tunnel stands an endless Universe of Love, Baba.

A Universe of gravitational *Love* pulling me into oneness with the . . .
moon,
traffic,
sunset,
surf.

There's no labor in my breath, no pain in my legs—
I am not the body jogging.

I AM FREE.

I AM!

Now, all moments, regardless of time or space,
run over with inner peace; my feet, bare or shod,
securely supported in Baba's love and grace—
my forever-present jogging companion.

Waterfall Shower, Love's Mist, Blessed In God's Grace!

Standing 'neath the shower's waterfall, steam spiraling into my lungs as
crystal pure streams carry the carnage of wasted cells
from my body, I feel the *Sunrise*
within my heart.

Golden-yellow rays silently slice through invisible channels,
bathing every cell in love and life.

Like bubbles in a bath, love and life lather foams
puffy white clouds floating through my mind.

Softened by the light, mind relaxes, releasing
muscles once tense and taut.

Tears of gratitude trickle from eyes delighted by the inner radiance—
a radiance intensifying as shower's pulsations
penetrate and soothe ever deeper.

Remnants of darkness and delusion crowd into passageways offering a
quick exit from the brilliance coursing through every cell.

My body shakes as my heart's appreciation compresses
the rising sun into a column of Light.

Extending down into the Earth of my root chakra and
high into the Heaven of my crown chakra,
a launching pad births.

A brilliant, scintillating cobalt-blue light rockets skyward,
exploding against my crown dome.

Stars burst within the peaceful solitude.
Darkness is shattered forever.

All without is within.
My face softens and glows, reflecting
the inner transformation.

To whom do I offer my salutations?

In which direction can I bow?

Where can I go where you are not?

Oh, Lord of Love,
With your infinite patience and compassion,
I offer my salutations,
My body, mind, heart, and soul
In whatever form You dance before me.

The *Sunrise* of my heart knows no dusk!

With your touch, it rose from the depths of my own being.
With your Grace, it will never set!

I Remember . . .

Oh, My Gurumayi
the glorious morning you entered me in all your radiant glory.

Oh, My Baba,
the night you opened my crown, ramming a blue shakti
lightning bolt down my spine.

Oh, My Bade Baba,
the afternoon you ignited the flame of my heart with yours.

Oh, My Lord Jesus,
the sunset you baptized and crucified me,
the night you took me to Heaven and Hell,
the ecstatic mOMent your index finger touched my forehead.

Oh, My Mother Mary,
the morning you lifted me and cradled me;
the time you entered me on request to feel, become *Compassion;*
when, in Amma's divine hug, I only felt YOU.

Oh, My Divine Amma,
hearing angelic voices in your loving hug,
dissolving into nothing in another hug, bliss-frozen, unable to move for hours.

Oh, My Master Yogananda,
the countless times your poetic expressions
filled my eyes with sweet tears of recognition.

Oh, My Mother Meera,
the night you massaged my spine as I slept and then
again, during darshan the next day.

Oh, My Masters of T'ai Chi and Reiki,
the many times you melted internal barriers,
giving me experiences of the truth, clearing my vision
to see what I needed to heal myself.

Oh, My Lord, in all your miraculous forms,
I remember and thank you
with my Life.

And to you, my friend, reflection of my very Self,
I thank you for being part of my life,
gifting me the
en***courage***ment
to be
me!

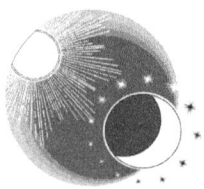

Dear Reader, now it's your turn to write. Use the blank space below. Try not to censor yourself.

Sit in your Poetic Temple, let your word waterfall flow.

Dearest heart and soul, I'm ready to hear what you want to share with me here and now.

"Every human heart's a flame of love burning to experience God within—Poetry fans the flame."

Known as the Magical & Mystical Fairy Tale Wizard & Poet, **Sensei Timothy** is a visionary educator, Sacred Sciences Master, *Tesla 3:6:9 Poetry Tyme* originator, Ordained Minister, Retired CPA, and the world's most prolific children's author (292+ stories).

Blending storytelling, meditation, qigong, Reiki and everything between, he inspires and empowers all ages to thrive through life's greatest challenges and live healthier, happier, soul-centered, poetic lives.

An Amazon #1 Best-Selling Author and Book Excellence Award Winner, he creatively weaves myth with mystery and fantasy with reality, sparking brilliance, creativity, and confidence—wiring children for success from conception to independence and beyond.

Through innovative books, courses, and programs like the "Sacred Sciences Alchemy Academy—turning teens into *Certified Personal & Business Black Belts*," he activates everyone to achieve their full potential.

Connect with Timothy: https://linktr.ee/timothystuetz.com

Chapter 19

From Loss/Lost to Light

Diane Wilbon Parks, PMP, Poet, Visual Artist

My Story

There is so much about me that you don't know. I imagine that sometimes you hide yourself in plain sight, too; holding the protective mask in place, just right, so that others cannot find you, even in the same shared spaces.

When my mother passed away, I stood in a corner for hours, pushing my face in between two walls, head leaning down, arms curved in front of my body. I nudged myself so far into the seam of those two waiting walls until I felt the whole room hugging me, like a new mother. Underneath the deep, dark edges of brokenness, I turned my back away from the world and screamed aloud, inside, "I am lost, and I don't want to be found."

There will be moments in your life and mine when we simply do not want to engage with others during our times of grief, loss, or hardship. However, I believe that it's critical to find healthy ways to cope with life's burdens. I've always entrusted the healing processes of praying and writing poetry to usher in the light. Perhaps poetry could be the place you offer yourself for healing.

There's so much about you that I don't know. I don't know what you've been through, nor what you've had to cope with, nor how often. But what I do know is what has worked for me. I hope, in some way, by sharing my story, you might see how poetry could help unlock your silence, your pain, and your suffering.

Poetry is where the haze of hope opened its arms, and the transformative process of healing took place in me. I trusted the practice of undressing my woes and worries in the body of a poem to repair and rebuild myself. With poetry, I could freely express whatever I couldn't say, or didn't want to say, and I chose whether I wanted to share it or not. Either way, it was cathartic to write about the painful things I went through.

Poetry will always be the silent place where I shed and restore, where I pull the shattered glass from imploding places, where I scream in a field of written words and paragraphs, where I run as far and as wide and as long as my thoughts will allow my poetic feet to roam—inside a poem.

Now that we've become more acquainted, I must admit that it wasn't easy to trust you with my pain. Still, it was necessary for you to understand the importance of helping you cope with whatever causes you to shelter your pain. Just imagine poetry as the kite lifting and soaring in the air, and that the kite is you and me. Once we let go of the string—the pain, the suffering—we move from the hard places into the places that allow us to leave but not forget, but rather, lift us out of our circumstances in order to move beyond the challenging times that keep us bound.

Poetry elevates my body, soul, and mind. I need it to heal, to grow, to cope, to release, to empower, and to beckon me back to light, love, and life. I hope it will do the same for you.

The Poems

The Page, the Poem and I

This poem does not have drawers,
it does not keep my mother's tongue
or my father's hope, it is not an
abandoned home leaning in from the past,

it is where I collapse onto the welcome
      mat of the page's altar,

it is where I transcribe silence into language,
      even these words, as thin as fishbones,
I squeeze them out as an offering.

I find my childhood summers here,
      yellow, with the sun's mouth wide open,
         and a lake of rivers gushing like two little girls,
I collect blue stones and every season here,
      and when it rains too hard and the lake
         is overcome with death and apology,
I twist into a butterfly to start over again.

This poem does not have drawers,
      it does not keep my mother's voice
         or my father's dream,
    it enters the front door of a page
    into the bright wilderness of my mind,
where I have spoken like a man,
      a voice of velvet baritone, spinning.

I have been lost, I have been
         a mad woman, a wife,
         a mother, a grandmother,
         a daughter

looking for her mother's eyes of understanding—
the first home I ever lived in – gone.

I have dislocated the black clouds,
walked through the souls of my own rivers
to carry the reflective waters back to
a new home to moisten the drought.

When I find my key, this pen, and walk into the door, this page,
this home,   the scripture of my soul dances,
            the sun rises, the church bell rings,

God enters this place too.

I have sinned here and have been baptized
and rinsed in the murky waters of a poem,

I have loved, and breathed inside its lungs
to relocate my soul,
to resurrect the life of a poet and a poem,
a body leaning in like a root, a punctuation on paper,
a branch with long fingers that hold the signatures
of my past, a family tree
of those who have gone
and those who I no longer see.

Even now, I lay everything here, my ink—
my black blood stretched across the page,
            I lay the moons of my black skin here,
                  my black thoughts too, I tilt into the spine of this page
                  and pluck vibrant wildflowers and purple plums
                  from the fields of a poem.
            I collect blue stones, my mother's songs, my father's hum
                  the long-stemmed silence of their ashed-blue breaths
                  and the sound of birds chirping—
                  where I find solace and home
                  in the body of a poem.

The Sun Comes into Me

When I turn Dark,
    the sun comes into me
      its fingers take deep breaths
        and open the blue-black curtains
          of my tongue where children hide
            their anger. I taste their disappointment,
              and return their bitter thoughts
                to candied song.

              When I turn Dark,
              I open my mouth
              and know that the
              moon sees the sun's
            reflection in me.
          I am half shaped,
        half mooned,
      half adult,
    half child
  painting
 yellow
circles,
 dripping
  as the paint
    s l o w dances
      d
        o
          w
            n
my yellow
painted throat,
Darkness
does not
return.

This eye reflects
a moon and a heart.
   When the sun comes
    into me, it stays,
  its fingers take
deep breaths
   and leave
        the gold, glittered gaze
        of windows opened—
    to cast light from
   the rise of my sun
and my rays.

Until This Becomes Old

May I have your wrinkles?
the ones that push in the direction of towards
the outcome of all things known at the end of reach,
but smell of youth.

May I walk with your thoughts to the four points of completion?
the place of God's voice, the whispering fold,
the place we celebrate the straights
that bend into forgiveness
and arrive at the most sacred place of worship and hope,

May I have all of your wayward thoughts from June
that lift up to see where your long troubles land?
and, in the fall, I will carry your windblown secrets,
light the world from blue bottles,
and re-appear inside the feet of lakes,
where answers see?

May I solace your white swaddle
and isolate into turning
to will my body to more than this?
to come back with multicolored wings
that love more than?

May I spread your wings and stop with you,
and watch your shadow walk on untouched grass?

May I lay beside your dreams
until this becomes old?
until we leave again?

May I run with your favorite colors,
and keep your echoes as my scriptures?
only air keeps you falling back to me.

we both push against the soft breeze
in pursuit of new.

A Place in the Sun

if you are here,
you have to imagine
that the sun is here too,
that it has lost the measurement of time,
that it has slipped underneath the white
beaded gown of bedded memories,
and found sleep on the other side,

you have to imagine
that the sun does not abandon darkness,
it temporarily finds shelter
in the cloak of your skin,
even in the hillside of blue mourning's,
listless and listening,
with a tinge of light blushing inward,
as if the world has moved on without you
or is waiting for you.

and like pain, the sun infiltrates
the deafening songs
of your surrendered body
with a deep lightning
that christens the poisons
plaguing your raised body,
each limb, each eye looking in,
where the holy rags are brightly lit
to catch stars plummeting from the sky
onto your bright, new path.

if you are here,
you have to imagine that the dance of thieves
who take your light and take your flight
are here too,
you have to remember that darkness is a
listener as well, you have to tell it to go

into the light,
that this deepening is temporary
and your madden mind loosening
from the screw's shadowed views
is something that always gather at the puckering,
where it, too, finds
a place in the sun.

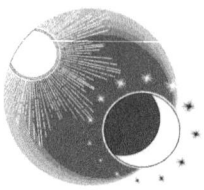

Dear Reader, now it's your turn to write. Use the blank space below. Try not to censor yourself.

Write a poem about a time when you experienced loss or felt lost and how you were able to find (the) light.

Diane Wilbon Parks is an accomplished poet, literary advocate, and visual artist. Diane has published two collections of poetry and a children's book. She was brought in as an expert consultant to the National Trust for Historic Preservation through a National Endowment for the Arts grant. She was a finalist in the Atlanta Review's international poetry contest. She celebrated the installation of one of her poems and artwork as a permanent sign at the Patuxent Research Refuge, North Tract in Laurel, Maryland. Diane is the founder of The Write Blend, a culturally diverse poetry circle, and a member of the Voices of Woodlawn, an ensemble of four poets reckoning America's past through poetry, and Diane's visual art. Her literary contributions have been featured nationally and internationally, on radio/blog radio, television, in newsletters, online journals and magazines, and in anthologies. Diane is a USAF Veteran. She resides in Maryland with her family.

Connect with Diane: https://www.facebook.com/diane.parks.790/

Chapter 20

Beyond This Place

Through Transformations

Lyn Veneziano Fry, MBA, MSGT Ret'd

My Story

Our kitchen was the center of all activities, especially in the winters of the 1950s. A cast-iron coal cook stove was the center of focus for the kitchen.

The stove provided the source of heat for our small four-room house. We heated water for Saturday baths, or nightly when Mom lined five or six of us up on the table, in order of age, to wash faces first, arms and hands, and lastly all legs and feet, after which we were off to sleep in one bedroom, two or three in each bed.

We dressed in the kitchen, meat from butchering was cut and packaged, Dad shaved, we did homework, crafts, ate, entertained relatives, hatched eggs, and started seedlings for the garden.

The stove was important for canning after the fall harvest. Hundreds of jars of fruits and vegetables, jams and jellies, etc., were processed and then stored in the cellar along with huge bins of potatoes and a large bin of coal, which was usually refilled several times over the winter.

To the right of the stove stood a metal baking cabinet with a kneading board, a roll-up door hiding the mixer, and a built-in flour sifter. Breads, pies, and egg noodles, which we helped unroll, were our favorites to watch Mom bake. She had a radio on top of this cabinet that she played most days. We loved hearing the music, and especially loved hearing Christmas carols.

The stovetop was black and always hot. It had several round griddles, a large oven, and always delicious aromas of something baking, simmering, or coffee brewing.

Our windows were single-pane. They frosted on the inside, giving us a place to carve out frosty art with our fingernails. The thin linoleum floors, especially upstairs, seemed to stay cold all winter.

The stove made the kitchen cozy. We had a coveted spot on the left side of the stove, which we shared with old newspapers and a stack of wood for kindling or burning that my siblings and I sat on.

We found this to be the best spot to remain part of the bustling kitchen activities while staying out of the way, and keeping warm on those frigid winter days in Drifting, Pennsylvania. We gathered Drifting got its name from the blustery winds that created massive snow drifts everywhere.

My favorite kitchen memories are sitting next to the stove and keeping warm with my siblings while my older sister, Rosemary, read stories to us. She was a few years ahead of us, already attending school. We were her audience while she practiced her reading assignments, and memorized poetry. I felt awe-struck as I fell in love with the magical worlds discovered within a book.

I couldn't get enough of the stories from those reading sessions. I eagerly anticipated attending school myself and was excited to learn to read and write, too.

Those early reading sessions inspired me to want to read, but more than that, to become a published author.

The Poems

Summer Breeze

The warm July breeze was a
delicate
and
sweet caress
on her bare skin
while gently lifting
the flowing fabric
of her summer dress.

It captured her thoughts,
reminding her of her lovers'
deliberate
and
stimulating touch
that transcended her
to a state
of pure delight.

The breeze continued
to swirl her skirt,
slipping underneath the flowing
material,
distracting her thoughts
with her body's response.

The loose fabric suddenly felt
restricting as her skin craved
for more exposure to this
titillating source
creating an innocent but
arousing
manipulation
of her body and soul.

The spontaneous pleasure of this
simple caress
erupted into
excitement for her senses,
enveloping her body
in a way that controlled her mind.

Standing there,
mesmerized in time and space,
she felt no boundaries
to her existence,
merely a creature content
in receiving joy
in this moment
of pure
delight.

Lost Dreams

In the memories of my
childhood
I see myself
in my innocence,
in naivety
I see my dreams.
I see excitement for the unknown.
Various possibilities are
swirling in my mind.

I ventured out
with optimism
and hope
into a world
of limitless opportunities
previously unviable.

The world was tough,
my innocence exploited
experience earned
through a pool of tears,
body and mind bruises,
scars,
but with
lessons of strength learned.

I got caught up in
distractions and
followed unknown paths,
falling often
getting up,
brushing off,
moving on to another day.

Many years pass and I recall that
list of dreams from my youth.
Those *lost* dreams
were no longer just perceptions of my youth,
they were part of the life I was living.
The life I dreamed
found me along the way.

Hello

The noise I keep feeding holds too many lies
It darkens a path I begin to despise.

Conversations within regarding problems to solve.
I pretend it's with the person involved.

It is unreal, though I think it truth
In my tortured state I look for proof.

I let it continue, but stop it I must
My faith is dwindling as is my trust.

The thundercloud above by others is felt
I live as if it's the fate I was dealt.

The rain comes down, spills from my eyes
I hear the noise, the room fills with my cries.

My body trembles from the storm inside
I want sleep to come in order to hide.

No sleep today, *no, not today.*
Can sadness ever be kept at bay?

Something pulls me to open the door
Go outside, life can be so much more.

I am approached with a smile, a kind word will do
Providing a calming caress as the storm leaves too.

I can see the sun, beauty in grass and trees
Suddenly I know how to be free.

Leaving the storm by changing my view
A kind word from a friend was all I needed from you.

That's all I needed, oh, such a pity.
Though I suddenly feel extremely happy and giddy.

Can this now be considered my norm
Since I have the power to avoid the storm.

It is in my control, I have a choice
Reach out, hear the *'hello'* of a friendly voice!

The Red Door

Bright red.
The door in front
of me catches my
attention.

It sits at the top of a dimly lit
staircase.

I am mesmerized.

Where does this bright beauty
lead
appearing out-of-place with
surroundings of muted grays
and dull earthy tones.

This red door beckons to me,
'ascend the stairs'.
There is a mystery to where
 the door leads.
What adventures await for one
brave enough?
I imagine wild possibilities.

Is it the color that intrigues
me?
The bold color itself surely
means something alluring?

Or is it the stairs partially
visible,
adding to the mystery and a
demand of strength
to go forward?

'Be brave', I hear.
'Be courageous,
take on the challenge, go toward the
unknown.'

"I will take it!"
I say to Ben, the artist and painter
of his latest watercolor,
The Red Door.

*In memory of the talented artist,
Ben Saggese
(1953 - 2024)

Dear Reader, now it's your turn to write. Use the blank space below. Try not to censor yourself.

When did you experience a red door that led to a transformation(s) and impacted your life in unexpected ways or taking you on an unexpected path? Were you brave enough to continue on in that direction?

Lyn Veneziano Fry grew up on a 160-acre farm in rural Central Pennsylvania. After she served in and retired from the military, she made her home in Lake Stevens, Washington. She enjoys traveling back to Pennsylvania, hiking around Puget Sound, the Cascade Range trails, and most recently, Mount Rainier.

After a diagnosis of osteoarthritis, Lyn made it her mission to strengthen her body by building muscle to remain pain-free and physically active. Besides writing, she loves everything Christmas, gardening, walking in nature, dancing, hiking, coordinating events, and continuing her love of exotic world travel with a recent trip to Egypt.

Lyn is a certified Law of Attraction Coach, Art of Feminine Presence coach/teacher, and CEO of Lightness of Spirit Personal Coaching.

Wanting to help others continue to be active as they age, Lyn became a certified strength trainer with MindfulOnlineGym.com.

Connect with Lyn: lightnessofspirit@gmail.com

Chapter 21

A Woman Emerged

Through Flames, Into Radiance

Jen Potter

My Story

My childhood was shaped by trauma. My mother, abusive, addicted, and lost in her own darkness, broke me down before I even knew who I was. When she finally abandoned our family, the damage she left behind ran deeper than words. And yet, in the midst of all that pain, my father tried to hold us together. He was the steady hand, the flicker of hope that reminded me life could still be gentle, even when it wasn't easy.

For years, I carried the weight of what she left behind—abuse, neglect, shame, and the deep wound of abandonment. I learned survival before I learned safety. I became the caretaker, the overachiever, the one who never slowed down, because stillness meant feeling the pain I wasn't ready to face.

But over the past several years, I stopped running. I turned toward the parts of myself I buried: the little girl who was silenced, the teenager who carried shame, the woman repeating cycles she didn't choose. I held them with compassion. I let the grief and the rage rise, and I didn't turn away.

I chose to change my life.

In that process, something beautiful began to take root. I learned to self-soothe, create safety inside my own body, and find joy, not in escape but in presence. I slowed down enough to be with my children, laugh with them, and show them a mother who is whole, not just surviving.

"You're safe now," I whispered to the little girl inside me. For the first time, she believed me. For the first time, I believed myself.

My writing deepened. My work became more authentic. My life began to feel like it was finally mine.

This isn't about erasing the past. It's about reclaiming myself after it. It's about turning broken pieces into a mosaic of truth, courage, and beauty.

If you have ever felt abandoned, silenced, or unworthy, I want you to know that you are not alone. Healing is possible. Wholeness is possible. Joy is possible.

These poems are my story, and they are also an invitation for you to begin your own journey back home to yourself.

The Poems

Beautiful Chaos

SLAMMING doors
Pounding in my memory
Shattered mirrors, crashing down
Scattered self-reflection across the floor
Piecing myself back together
Slowly. . .

While lost in the chaos
Guarded walls
I have to protect myself
Protect my mind. . .

Closed tightly
I can't let anyone in
Protect my heart. . .

What do you know?

I just CAN'T. . .

You just DON'T get it!

I WON'T!

Falling short
False promises
Scars in my mind
Scars across my body
AFRAID!

Always on high alert
Allow myself to be vulnerable? Ha
How can I just allow myself to trust someone not to hurt me?

How can my soul settle down
Enough to allow someone in?
Fear. . .

Fear of judgment
Greater than the fear
Of facing the truth. . .
Because the truth is. . .

I actually *do* not know how. . .
How can I let my guard down?

No one understands why it's so hard living in this mind that is racing
Uncontrollable noise. . .
Chaos

Why can't I just get the noises
in my head to soften?
Screaming from the bellows of my belly
I am searching for safety
An entire life of searching. . .
Searching. . .
Searching. . .

Chasing the Storm

Through the chaos beauty lies
Heart racing. . .
Wind swirling inside a belly of fire
I crave the rush of the water
Like the touch of skin against mine

Excitement. . .

Chaos. . .

Like a perfectly formed wave
Crashing down
Like a heartbeat
Beautiful disaster
Will I catch it?

Each wave different from the next
They are unique like the soul
If I miss my chance I may never experience it again

The love is overwhelming
Waves crashing
Too much to handle
A mind that is extreme

Thoughts quickly run through my brain
Passion ignites
The presence of the rush comes over me
Falling into the depth of the ocean
I can't break away
I'm addicted to the *chaos*
Adrenaline through my veins
Heart racing out of my chest

Passion of like I've never felt

Beautiful disaster

Calm

Touching

Souls intertwined
Love like I've never experienced
Love like the rush of waves
A soul like the serene landscape I crave

She is a Rose

Oh beautiful rose
Bringing beauty and life to everything around her
She grew amongst others in a bush that weathered through the storms
Survived the pouring rain and powerful winds of life
Yet, she found a way to radiate brighter

Growing stronger and more resilient
Her light ignited passion in those around her
Soft
Delicate
Vibrant

Carefully selecting the soul to protect her
Allowing her heart to be plucked from the bush
Powerful
Independent
Beautiful

She needed you to care for her
Nourish her
Love
Passion
Understanding

She allowed you in
Supported and complemented you
Intertwined her love with yours

She watered you with her love
Seeds of herself sprinkled into a family
Wanting to watch you grow
What once was flourished
Began to dwindle
Giving so much of herself away
Not allowing herself to shine the way she once did

Slowly her petals started to change
She still *chose* you
Sharing pieces of herself with you
Needing more
Never giving up
She was slowly dying

Trying to replenish her soul
Needs being unmet
But not expressing herself
Not allowing her true light to shine
She could no longer love you the way she once did

As the petals began to fall, she grasped at holding on
This once beautiful rose has been torn down
Plucked
Her color faded
Impossible

She can not be saved
Time can not be reversed
She knew what must be done
She must allow herself to evolve

Sinking back inside the dark unknown soil that she once grew from
Surrendered
Vulnerable
Afraid

Hidden in the darkness a new seed is born
As the seedling blossoms

Remember how fragile her heart is
but do not forget the storms she endured

For every flower that allows herself to die
Know that the rebirth will be stronger than before

Divine Transformation

Hidden raging riptides
She is swirling in this moment of chaos hidden from the surface
Rooted desires to be free
Embracing the wildly majestic ocean
She seeks a beautifully curated transformation
Happiness flickers from within like a firefly
As stars linger
Across the deep night jungle sky
Calming thoughts of the unknown
Her beautiful heart beats
For long lost sunshine of serene skies
Her sun-kissed soul craving more of this life
She feels tranquility take over as the magic of the universe divinely
orchestrates
Water falls onto her skin
Healing her wounds she has lived a thousand lives
How did she get here?
Choosing a life to be

Wild
Wise

Free…

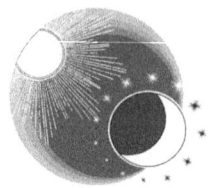

Dear Reader, now it's your turn to write. Use the blank space below. Try not to censor yourself.

You have journeyed through words written from my own healing—from the raw places of trauma to the rebirth of light and self-love. Now, it's your turn to put pen to paper.

Take a deep breath. Let yourself feel whatever rises. Then, respond to this:

"What part of my story still feels like a scar I hide, and what might happen if I let it speak?"

You can write a poem, a letter, or just a fragment of a thought. It doesn't have to be perfect—only real. Even a whisper of truth carries its own beauty.

If you feel stuck, begin with one of these lines and let it carry you:

"I remember when. . ."
"The silence felt like. . ."
"If my younger self could speak, she would say. . ."
"Healing, to me, feels like. . ."

Jen Potter runs several businesses, each rooted in creativity, community, and connection. She's a mom of three, author, surfer, and new skateboarder who thrives on adventure and soulful living. At the heart of everything she does is a mission to help women reconnect with their divine feminine energy, reclaim their voices, and design lives that feel aligned and free.

Going through this journey through trauma, healing, and transformation has shaped Jen into more than just an entrepreneur or guide. She's living proof that resilience and joy can coexist. Whether catching waves, skating at the park, or writing words that spark reflection, she brings a vibe that's bold, real, and unapologetically her. "Life is about collecting experiences, expressing truth, and radiating light. And my purpose is simple: to walk beside others as they rise, reclaim, and shine."

Connect with Jen: https://www.instagram.com/jen_liveyourbestlife/

Chapter 22

The Unbroken Thread Home

Words from the Heart

Elizabeth Kipp, Stress Management and Historical Trauma Specialist

My Story

I didn't realize I was a poet until that part of me insisted on being heard.

It didn't arrive politely, waiting for permission. It burst forth from underground, shaking the earth beneath my quiet exterior.

I grew up in a home where words followed rules. You either responded immediately or stayed silent. And if you couldn't find the "right" answer, silence was the safer choice.

"Children are to be seen and not heard."

"That's enough—be quiet."

The message was clear: my words were dangerous. My voice was expendable.

But I found refuge in other voices—Dr. Seuss, William Blake, John Donne, Shakespeare's sonnets, and more—each a secret portal out of my confines. I read as if my breath depended on it. Maybe it did.

I wrote according to my teachers' instructions—boxed in tightly.

Over time, I learned to swallow my words, bury them deep, and act as if they weren't there.

I didn't realize how much poetry saved my life until the only thing I had left of my wits were the words.

Words heal. They seal safety into the dark when I've lost my footing and everything else. And there are the words, painting away, lighting up the black shroud surrounding me.

Recovering from experimental surgery in a sprawling teaching hospital, surrounded by strangers in white coats, I felt utterly alone lying in my bed.

I'm walking a tightrope here in the dark. There's thick black ink surrounding me in all this pain. There's no end in sight. But I have this thin silvery cord beneath my feet, straddling between here and there, wherever 'there' is. I just need to stay balanced, one step at a time, and traverse this space - madness to my left, a heart attack to my right. The world is a knife's edge.

I kept moving forward, one step at a time, on a path no one could walk for me, while the voice from my heart whispered words that pulled me along.

Come this way. Here. And here. And now here.

Here was an unbroken spirit, Divine intelligence, leading me on with the sweetest, most hope-filled words.

Since then, I promised to listen to my words and give them air to spread out before me on the canvas of life.

They keep me alive, and perhaps they'll do the same for you.

Now, poetry awakens me at night, rushes through me in traffic, and falls into my lap like a gift I didn't order but can't refuse. I learned to trust it.

Trust—because I know what it's like to wear an impostor's smile while unraveling inside.

I understand how invisible pain can be.

I know the way a single word, honestly spoken, can pierce that invisibility and offer a healing space of safety and connection.

"I see you. You're still here. You're not alone."

My poems are for all of us holding a thousand feelings in a sigh.

They're for anyone walking their thin silvery cord in the dark, praying for a guide to lead them home.

Words that rise from the deepest part of us are the unbroken thread home.

May we follow them again and again.

The Poems

Here's to giving voice to the invisible struggle so many people live with but rarely speak aloud. Maybe we appear fine on the outside while silently unraveling on the inside. Quiet desperation can grip those who feel trapped, unseen, and unsure how to ask for help. I want to help break the silence around mental health, suicide, and the aching need to be witnessed without judgment. May we learn to look beneath the surface, recognize the subtle signs, and remember that behind every smile might be a story untold, waiting to be witnessed, and pointing the way home to the heart.

Impostor Smile

I need a little help here, but I
don't know what to say.
No one wants to talk about
the darkness, so I smile the
impostor's way.

I'm kind of in a corner here.
The walls are closing in.
I'm coming off in layers, and
I'm drowning in this wind.

No one's here to help me,
and I don't know what to do.
I'm sending out these subtle
signs as I quietly come
unglued.

I need a little help here, but
the words get in the sway.
No one sees what I'm trying
so desperately not to say.

I know I'm in here
somewhere, but it feels like
I've gone.
I'm a ghost in my own skin,
holding on for so long.

Don't tell me to be stronger;
I'm already breaking (far
too) well.
If you could only just sit
here in the silence and
notice where I fell.

Won't someone come to my
rescue in this imprisoned reverie?
Help me see there's
something else besides this
last resort and final delivery.

Neurodi Verse

I'm not befuddled.
I just see the world sideways
with subtitles, in multidimensions,
and sometimes with
interpretive dance,
frequencies wide-open, full
throttle.

I'm not befuddled.
My brain's just. . .jazz.
Improv all day,
with a side of interpretive
spreadsheet.
I don't "zone out"
I time-travel mid-
conversation.
You said "weather"
and suddenly I'm designing
a utopia where clouds sing
affirmations.

I live in layers.
Peel one back and find a
symphony,
peel another. Hello,
existential wormhole.
It's not chaos. It's
kaleidoscopic clarity.

I think in triplicate.
And sideways.
And occasionally in whale song.
And then I cross-reference it
with dreams
I had it at 3:42 a.m. on a

Wednesday in 1997.
(I took notes. Probably in
crayon.)

You say "simple."
I say "symbiotic system of
soul signals."
Tomato, tomahto.
I am not befuddled.

I'm a glittery glitch in a
linear world
bedazzled by nuance,
allergic to small talk,
and fluent in subtext.

I feel you from across the
room,
even if I'm hiding in the
bathroom
with noise-canceling
headphones
and an emotional support
snack.

Structure? Yes.
I'm a cathedral of Post-it
notes and rituals,
an ocean that alphabetizes
its own waves.

Sometimes I disappear
but not because I'm lost.
I'm just recalibrating. . .
or untangling a metaphysical
slinky.

I'm not befuddled.
I'm imminent.
I'm me.
On purpose.
In rhythm.
A little offbeat, maybe
but dancing just the same.

So no, I won't apologize for
my sparkle,
my sideways glance at
reality,
or the way I hold a thousand
feelings
in the space of a sigh.

I'm not befuddled.
I'm a limited-edition neural
mixtape
with bonus tracks,
unexpected plot twists,
and occasional interpretive
sneezing.

Just know, I'm not
befuddled.
I'm becoming.

And isn't that the point?

Threaded in Stardust

(a return to the wild)

Come back to the beginning,
that first impulse, that
emanation of you
before the weight of the
world crashed in on you.
Release all that remains
unresolved in you
and come back.

There is nothing to fix,
no riddle to solve,
no further inputs needed,
only presence in the breath.

Stay in the whisper of the
now and come back.
Come back to the pulse
beneath the noise,
the hush beneath the hurry,
the knowing that never left
you.

Come back to you,
threaded in stardust,
who remembers how to
listen,
who trusts the quiet,
who speaks in the language
of stillness
and belongs to the holy
rhythm of this moment.

What is here,
what has always been here,
is pure love,
the original emanation,
the unbroken thread,
the truth of you.

Come back
again and again
into love.

Threads of silver light drift
through you,
defining the very weave of
your being.

Breath is your constellation.

Stillness is your song.

Come back
and remember
you never left
love.

Lighthouse:
Zero Point of Infinite Return

(you're a wild, holy rhapsody of brilliance)

Shame on the brain - will
whip up shade faster than a
tornado in Kansas.
It'll send you scrambling for
cover, ducking your own
brilliance,
forgetting you were born lit.

But here's the thing:
you're not a paper lantern
swaying on someone else's
porch.

You're the damn lighthouse,
built to stand in storms,
built to beam,
built to call the lost home.

Self-love isn't a whisper; it's
the infinite return. It's
looking in the mirror and
being struck with awe at
the truth of your magnificence.

It's looking shame dead in
the eye and saying,
"I see your pain. Come
climb into my heart and be
healed for once and for all."

It's refusing to shrink just
because your shine makes
someone squint.
It's knowing you are not a
sum of your mistakes

but the wild, holy rhapsody
coursing through you.

Unconditional means no
deal-making,
not when you're "better,"
not when you've "earned it,"
not when you "get there,"
wherever that might be.

It means loving the salt in
your tears,
the cracks in your voice,
the faltering parts just
learning the way.

The lighthouse, penetrating
the deepest night, smothered
in the darkest cloak.

You're the damn lighthouse.
Let the waves crash.
Let the sky split open.

Stay lit.
Because when you love
yourself without conditions,
you're not surviving the
storm,
you are the weather,
and the eternal beacon
burning
the zero point of infinite
return.

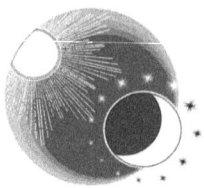

Dear Reader, now it's your turn to write. Use the blank space below. Try not to censor yourself.

Let your words flow.

If I could follow the unbroken thread of my own words without fear, I would _____.

Elizabeth R. Kipp is a Stress Management and Historical Trauma Specialist, Trauma-Trained and Yoga-Informed Addiction Recovery Coach, Ancestral Clearing Practitioner, and best-selling author of *The Way Through Chronic Pain: Tools to Reclaim Your Healing Power.* She is a long-time seeker of truths with a foot in both the spiritual and scientific worlds. Her life experiences and training enable her to bridge the gap between these two worlds.

Her deep connection to the spiritual world, including her ancestors' spirits, supported her through multiple surgeries, decades of prescribed medications, and a long, persistent search for modalities to help her heal.

Now, in long-term recovery, Elizabeth guides people to unleash their healing power. She uses Ancestral Clearing, Yoga, meditation, and other powerful tools to help people release their past burdens and live a life free from suffering.

Connect with Elizabeth: https://elizabeth-kipp.com/resources/

Chapter 23

Teardrops Bathe My Heart
Healing Grief Through Rhythmic Reverence
Jean Voice Dart, Expressive Arts Therapist

"The expressive act, whether through rhythm, imagery,
voice, or metaphor, is the healing force. You don't just describe pain;
you move through it, sing with it, paint it, weep it, and release it."
~Jean Voice Dart

My Story

I didn't realize my life would change forever when I timidly pushed on that door.

I'm different. Will they accept me?

As it opened, it creaked with a familiar groan, revealing a space that hummed with the quiet chaos of teenage life.

Old fluorescent lighting buzzed overhead, casting a pale glow over rows of mismatched desks etched with years of doodles, initials, and cryptic messages carved during moments of boredom or angst. Many carried an underbelly of sticky rebellion—the gum graveyard, a testament to the quiet defiance of youth. A cluttered teacher's desk sat nearby, guarded by a fortress of coffee mugs, paper stacks, and a drooping flower in a small vase.

Troubled teens slumped against their chairs like tired travelers. The air carried a familiar mixture of pencil shavings, teen cologne, and the faint scent of tater tots and sloppy joes wafting from the cafeteria.

"Hey, guys. Today is the day."

"Don't remind me. My palms are already sweating."

"No sweat. Just write something short and deep. Like, the clock ticks. Life ends."

"Wow. You're so cheerful, Joe. Your writing should be on a Hallmark card."

Harmonious laughter followed Rick's comments, and a creaky protest announced our teacher's entrance. Everyone quickly positioned themselves and opened their notebooks.

"Good morning, class. Alright. You know what to do." She sat behind her desk.

Eyes darted around the room. Whispered flirtations accompanied the determined efforts of my creative classmates.

"Fifteen minutes left. Finish up."

We furiously scribbled, releasing our emotions through pen and ink.

We were different, yet the same, a mosaic of personalities: awkward, brilliant, distracted, and hopeful. Each of us danced to the shared rhythm of adolescence.

Quiet concentration blanketed our heads, like a creative canopy.

The moment arrived. I breathed in my truth.

I'm a poet. Do they see me? Do they hear me?

Holding my handwritten paper, I stood before my peers, readied myself for the journey, and released my deepest feelings through the spoken word. My entire life shifted from that point forward. Grief took flight, and memories morphed into melodies. I forged through pain and paused in the stillness of my heart.

After seventeen years of feeling fear, doubt, and shame, I finally recognized my tears as much more than despair, sadness, and sorrow. Grief and tears were not something to fear. Grief is love's echo, and tears are my way of expressing creative flow, connection, and courage.

My high school poetry class was not just a classroom; it was a transformation chamber, bringing liberation and transcendence. Yet, we each have our transformation chambers: the chambers of our hearts.

Healing occurs through this basic process.

1. **Feel:** Find a quiet space to feel your mental, emotional, physical, and sociological pain. Fully face and embrace your feelings.

2. **Reveal:** Express your feelings through the rhythmic reverence of words (write, read aloud, share with others privately or in a community).

3. **Heal:** Continue to express yourself, allowing teardrops to bathe your heart. Power lies in partnership. Invite joy and gratitude to accompany you through pain. Share your experiences with trusted friends, family, or professionals.

Let's walk together and heal through the expressive arts.

The Poems

I invite you to join me in this symbiotic relationship between writers and readers. Here is my offering of creative transformation. I've chosen these poems especially for your healing journey. Please let the words touch you deeply as tears bathe your heart. Read them, speak them, and embody them. Each poem carries a rhythmic reverence, a magical cadence for healing. And so do you. You are rhythm and rhyme. It is within you. Before reading the poem aloud, take a deep breath. Look within your heart. You are a courageous, creative conqueror, ready for the journey—ready to discover, identify, and release blocked feelings and embrace joy. I applaud you.

Endlessly Flowing

Too busy.
Too stressed.
Too tired.
No rest.
Endlessly flowing,
Rapidly going.

Too little.
Too much.
Too absent.
No touch.
Endlessly flowing,
Rapidly going.

I awake from a dream.
It's a powerful stream.
Too busy.
Too stressed.
Too tired.
No rest.

Endlessly flowing,
Rapidly going.
Lovingly glowing,
Quietly knowing.
Flowing and growing.
Yet, I begin slowing.

Where am I?
What is this?
How can I get through?
Who am I?
When will you?
Why is there no clue?

A kind voice emerges
Converges, and glows.
Re-worths me,
Unearths me,
Rebirths me.
It knows.

Grieving,
Weaving,
Believing,
Conceiving.

Give and you live.
Give and forgive.
Give and you find
All you seek.

Give and let go.
Give and you know.
Giving is not
For the fearful and weak.

Give what?
Give who?
Give now?
Give where?
Give up.
Give in.
Give over.
With care.

Give all.
Give love.
Give you.
Give more.
You fall.
Get up.
Rise up
From the floor.

Endlessly flowing,
Rapidly going.
Now I am knowing,
Glowing and
Showing.

Keep giving.
Keep living.
It's alright to fall.
When you give to yourself.
And to It.
It is all.

Different, Yet the Same

Different.
Yes, you are.
Your oddity makes me smile.
I love you.
Yet, your words bring tears.
Different.
Sharp, yet soothing.

Different.
Soar.
Splash.
Ready to crash.
The dark night awakens to the dawning day,
And my heart opens to the sun of you.
You radiantly shine and warm me.
I hold your gift,
Then lose it,
And miss it when it's gone.
You offer it again.

Different.
The hurt comes.
What once attracted, now repels.

Different.
Can it be as it once was before?
My outstretched arms
Long for the warmth of divine love.
Yet, I am spinning in the spiral of life.

Different.
I want to be free.
Climbing mountains.
Running in the wind.
Floating with the stars.
Leaping across a vast lake of tears,

And resting safely upon the shore.
You are there with me.
You carry me when I fall.

Different.
One last time, I try.
Seeking wisdom, truth, and love.
People.
Books.
Words.
Images.
Searching,
Searching,
Seeking life.

Until that moment.
That day.

I look up from this chapter of life
And I finish.
I stop searching.
I stop seeking.
I start seeing.
I stop looking and surrender,
Falling deeply into the mirrored illusion of life.

I see myself.

I am here now.
I am who I seek.
Thank you, God.
It is me.
For you never left me.
It was I who was lost.
It was I who I wanted to see.
It was I who I left behind.
I wasn't seeking you,
For you are always here at my side, loving me.
Thank you for helping me find myself.

I am the blazing sun warming my heart.
I am the rugged mountain I venture to climb.
I am the wind, urgently pushing me forward.
I am the stars brilliantly illuminating my life.
I am the vast lake of tears here for me when I need to feel my pain.
I am the mirrored image of illusions, guiding me to the truth.

Thank you, God, for patiently waiting.
I look into the mirror now,
Seeing nothing but reflections of divine love.
I see you.
I see me.
I see the blessings of life.

Different, yet the same.
Hand in hand, we walk together.
The cold, ocean waves wash upon us,
Our hands raised up to the heavens.
Together we journey forward,
And I am forever grateful for the blessing of this day.
You are always with me.
I am home.

Teardrops Bathe My Heart

Teardrops
Bathe my heart,
Filling it with gratitude.
The sacred sound
Purifies my eternal being.
I am home.

You stand nearby.
Your whispers of wisdom
Wash upon me like the wind.

They comfort me.
Now and always.
I am never alone.
Never alone.

Teardrops
Bathe my heart.
Memories of you
Walking beside me,
Always there,
Opening my eyes.

Cold.

Teardrops bathe my heart.
Sitting in my warm home,
Surrounded by framed memories.
Happy times.
Smiles and hugs.

Loneliness,
I hate you.
Loneliness,
I love you.

Why do you follow me?
Why do you tease me?

The frosty air awakens my lungs.
My aging fingers tap, slip, and rest.
The youthful agility dissolves
As I watch the years fly by.

Older now.
Aching.
Shaking,
Waking,
Taking time to heal.

Teardrops bathe my heart.
Loving memories tug at me.
Where are they now?
Grown and gone.

A metal cane rests against the door.
A warm blanket cradles and comforts,
And I sit in solace,
Surrendering in serenity,
Rocking to remembered rhythms.
Humming to unwritten melodies.

Teardrops
Bathe my heart.
Yet, here at my side
Is the Comforter.
Always with me.
Empowering me.
Whispering gentle words
Of wisdom and peace.

"Always remember
You are the joy.
Always remember,
You are the love.
Always remember.
You are the Light.

"Not a pretender.
Not a contender.
Now wrapped
In splendor
With words
So tender.
Always remember.
Surrender.
Surrender.

"Yes, you did.
Yes, you will.
Yes, you are.

"Follow the call.
Follow your heart.
Follow the call.
Never depart."

Teardrops
Bathe my heart.
Gratitude washes over me.
My muscles ache,
My eyelids close.

A burning fire
Pulses through my veins,
Emblazoned within me.
A tear drips down my cheek,
Warming me
With love.

Who am I to be so loved?
Who am I to be so blessed?

Thank you.
Thank you.
I am finished.
I am yours.
I am done.
I surrender.

Teardrops
Bathe my heart
With humility and grace.
I am whole,
And purified
By your embrace.

I am loved,
Always.
And heaven
Is forever
Mine.

Grounded in Grief, Flowing with Grace

I see you there.
Your sound embraces me.
Your song fulfills me.
Your melody tiptoes through my heart.

I love you always.
I see you always,
I hear you always.

Fluttering wisps of wonder fill the air.
Pictures dance before my eyes
And push down upon my brow.
Grief bubbles up into my throat.

I swallow it.

Walking.
Stopping.
Thinking.
Sitting in your chair.
Touching.
Smiling.
Sighing.
Feeling the softness of you.
Seeing you in the textures and smells of the room.

No.
No.
Stop.

It's alright, dear one.
It's alright.
I must go.
I will love you always.

You are the flame within my heart.
Burning away unnecessary chatter.
Leaving only pure euphonious tones.

Wasted moments now embraced.
I leave this place.

I walk.
I run.
I dance.
I spin within this limitless playground.
No walls.
No floors.
No rooms.
I soar throughout the heavenly worlds.
I flee.
I fly.
I float.
I rise above the haunting melody of you.

You are the suffering,
The pain,
The joy,
The fire that stirs me to be more.
See more,
Give more.
Live more.

I am gone.
And yet you are here.
Tears fill my eyes.
Pain grips my heart.
Fisted fingers relentlessly squeeze.

Holding,
Clutching.
A desperate attempt.
Each finger slowly moves,
Successively releasing me
Into the soothing sounds of the universe.

Freedom wets my lips.
Hmmmm.
Hmmmm.
My heart explodes with joy.

I cannot go.
I must not stay.
So, I dance.

I dance for you,
For us,
For me,
For the world.

I listen to the beckoning call of the hawk.
I sing to the music of the spheres.
I waltz to the mellifluous melodies.

Urging me,
Purging me,
Pushing me.
Keep moving,
Keep dancing.

"Follow me.
Follow me,"
He whispers.

Pain flows from my heart,
An incessant,
Convalescent,
Effervescent release.

Flow.

I look to the heavens.
The sun beats upon my brow.
It opens my eyes,
Bathing me in goodness,
Showering me with kindness.

I breathe in the blessings
Ahhhh.
Ooooo.

I spin,
I twirl,
I prance,
I dance upon the clouds.
I miss the wet ground beneath my feet.
Forever flying free.

It's alright, dear one.
I am gone.
Yet we are here together.
Stop now.
Gasp.
Pause.
Breathe.

Shhh.
Shhh.
The ambient silence
Orchestrates the moment.

Grace.

I am gone.
Yet,
You will always remain
In my heart.

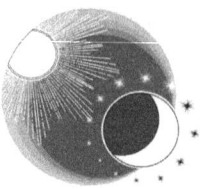

Dear Reader, now it's your turn to write. Use the blank space below. Try not to censor yourself.

Your heart is speaking to you, talking about its transformation from grief to joy. What is it saying?

Jean Voice Dart, M.S., RMT, is a multiple international best-selling author, expressive arts psychotherapist, coach, and teacher who navigated through grief, trauma, and chronic pain, upleveling her life from stressed to blessed. She has witnessed a lifetime of miraculous transformations, helping others feel, reveal, and heal through the arts.

Having lost multiple family members to suicide, Jean hosts The Wellness Universe's "Take My Hand Support Series" for mental wellness, suicide awareness, and education. Those working with Jean spark creative flow and gain effective, practical strategies to manage life challenges through the expressive arts (art, music, writing, movement, and drama).

She conducts private sessions, workshops, and classes worldwide. When Jean is not expressing herself through poetry and the creative arts, she is walking near the Pacific Ocean with her husband Matt and their dog, Pumpkin.

Connect with Jean: https://www.jeanvoicedart.com

Chapter 24

Healing Haiku

A Poetic Approach to Process Layers of Loss

Dinahsta *"Miss Kiane"* Thomas, MSW
Poet, Performer, and Safe Space Facilitator

My Story

I thought he was the one, but he was a lying, manipulating bastard. What does that make me? I thought she'd live to see 100. Where is home now? Watching your dog be put down is cruel. God, where are you?

My unanswered questions and inconsolable thoughts recreated a war scene straight out of Braveheart. It was an analytical battle between the right and left sides of my brain, complete with gore, guts, and chaos. While back at home in the heart, emotions of emptiness, confusion, numbness, and rage fought fiercely like teenage girls pulling hair, scratching skin, and tearing clothes.

There were no rules in these war zones, only a pounding headache and a tightness in my chest. And settling in my gut was the carnage of it all.

I experienced loss before. I wasn't unfamiliar with the effects of grief, but what do you do when loss is multiplied and grief is exponential? My life was filled with Goliaths—the threat of homelessness, the death of my canine companion of 15 years, the new title of adult orphan, the man who broke my heart with a smile, and health concerns that I could no longer control. Like David in the Bible, I needed a small, smooth stone to defeat the things that were bigger than me.

Journaling and free writing have always been my method of choice for processing difficult times, but during this season of layered loss, I was inspired by a more structured poetic form—the haiku.

Haiku is a traditional Japanese poem consisting of only three lines, with each line containing a syllabic pattern of 5-7-5. In my effort to manage my giants, I created my own poetic form called the healing haiku[1] in which I string three standalone haiku together to form one poem with three parts: the problem, the process, and the pivot. This was my small, smooth stone.

The first stanza, or "the problem," articulates an emotional angst, a troubling issue, or even a haunting question like "God, where are you?" Due to the Herculean nature of the thoughts and feelings within, this may be the most challenging stanza to write. The writer is encouraged to sit with the source of their pain, whittle away fluff, and identify truth in its rawest form.

The second part of the healing haiku is "the process." This stanza describes what the writer is feeling and/or doing as a result of the issue presented. Most of us find ourselves here in the dash of it all, the liminal space between the beginning and the end. This portion of the poem provides a behind-the-scenes peek at the healing journey.

The third and final stanza is called "the pivot," where the author identifies a positive resolve, has a change in perspective, or experiences a spiritual repair. This haiku may take time to write because healing takes place in a crockpot, not a microwave.

---

1. The Healing Haiku is a combination of a sequence haiku and a triptych poem where three distinctive but related parts are put together to form one poem.

When your life is filled with overwhelming thoughts, unanswered questions, and unregulated emotions, you have to find a way to reduce the Goliath-sized situations so you can slay your giant(s) and heal! David used a stone and a sling-shot. I use paper and a pen!

The Poems

Grieving Brody

Your eyes strong and weak.
Who knew death could be a gift?
Wait! I take it back!

Grief harasses me
Demanding my company
Leaving me alone.

Joy-rich memories
Float like stars in my midnight
Dawn will rise again.

Seasons Change

Baron brown branches
Emerald green grass stripped naked
Winter darkness lurks

Scarves clothe collarbones
Exhales freeze in mid-air and
Bears sleep underground.

Till one day life stirs
Sun-filled skies melt frozen breaths
Royal green pastures revealed.

Time Hurts and Heals

Promises of love
Fantasies of forever
With words, you hitched me.

I have been waiting
Waiting for your words to live
some words fly, yours died.

Time can hurt and heal
24 months passed you by
Now my healed heart flies.

I've Been Writin' These Poems. . .

I've been writin' these poems to convert this tangled chain of trauma
around my neck into a timeless piece of jewelry. . .
abracadabra this yoke into a string of pearls
a family heirloom of resilience and rarity
because just like the oyster,
my poetry is the nacre that protects me from my soul's enemies.

I've been writin' these poems to lasso my runaway heart
penning her down to a paper hospital bed
where the IV ink drips into hollow veins
medicinal words give voice to pain
so her healing can begin.

I've been writin' these poems as an exercise of faith
believing that these bars would extricate me from these bars
set my soul free and make history
generational curses destroyed and reversed
re-versing the soundtrack of my legacy.

Just like my tenacity,
pearls form as a result of an audacity to choose life
over and over and over again.

I've been writin' these poems
leaving bread crumbs for unicorns like me
to find their way back home.

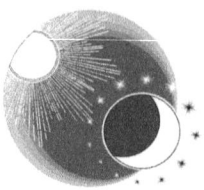

Dear Reader, now it's your turn to write. Use the blank space below. Try not to censor yourself.

What questions, thoughts, or emotions have become a giant(s) in your life, and what steps are you taking to reduce that giant(s) to a size manageable for your healing process to begin or continue?

Dinahsta "Miss Kiane" Thomas is a social worker, spoken word artist, and safe space facilitator. With a desire to fuse her social work profession with her poetry passion, Miss Kiane founded *The Inkwell,* a nonprofit that nurtures healing, awareness, and self-love through reflective writing programs, journal drives, and community wellness education. She also helps emerging artists share their voices with confidence through her freelance coaching services. Her work spans corporate spaces, classrooms, and communities where she inspires growth through soft skills training, teambuilding workshops, and reflective writing circles. Author and co-author of several poetic collections, Miss Kiane has graced stages from the Library of Congress to the L.A. Breakfast Club. In whatever setting Miss Kiane finds herself in, she facilitates a safe space filled with emotional awareness, creativity, and healing.

Conect with "Miss Kiane": https://linktr.ee/misskiane

Chapter 25

A New Kind of Poetry

Laura Di Franco

"It's your job to make me feel something. It's the only job of a writer."

You wanna know just how much I loved hearing that from a writing coach? A lot. And I say it to every single author and poet who moves through my world. I love staring at my Zoom screen as most of the room nods in acknowledgement.

"Again! Again!"

As I watched Jeff Young perform a poem about music one night at an open mic, and heard the shouting from the back of the room, those exact words went through my mind.

Again! Again! Please, take me on that journey with you again! Let me run around to the entrance and hop on that ride again! This is a thrill! Hands up!

He, and many poets since, helped me fall in love with spoken word. I sit in the now so deeply grounded that I forget where I am for a moment. When a moment helps me do that I feel like I've succeeded, whatever that means.

"What does success mean to you?" You've been asked this before, right?

This so-in-the-moment-I-forgot-where-I-was thing has only happened to me once or twice before. There was one time during lovemaking (yep, it was that good) and another time in the presence of my first real waterfall in Hawaii.

But poetry, when it does this to me—that's true ecstasy. It's a full-body presence so full and complete that anxiety dissolves into a puff of smoke, disappearing into the flames, and I'm left with joy, its iridescent glitter-sparkle oozing from my skin, eyes, and smile—that involuntary lean toward the stage tugging me closer.

Mmm, mmm, mmm, yes please, more of that. I'm snapping so much my fingers ache. I can't snap enough, so the "Whoohoo!" escapes my throat.

This book was so full of these moments for me. Over and over I thought:

Wow, you showed me a piece of your soul. Thank you. Now I know I'm not alone. And that knowing suddenly has more staying power. Thank you. Thank you. Thank you.

And today I thank the gift that is poetry. Poetry is a precious gift of soul-filled words, of get-me-back-into-my-body moments that remind me where all the healing magic happens. Thank you for healing me. Thank you for helping my friends process, integrate, and express.

100 Poems & Possibilities for Healing.

Actually, there are more than 100 possibilities, because sometimes it's one line in a poem that helps you connect. Sometimes it's a word, a phrase, or a stanza that speaks to you. Sometimes you fall in love with a sentence so deeply you want to write an entire memoir from it.

YES! Let these lines be prompts for your soul, dear reader! Every prompt offered by these poets is an invitation. Be curious! Pause before you turn the page. Pause and breathe and write!

Feeling restless, judgmental, or some other kind of resistance or reaction inside? Fantastic! That right there is the possibility you have for healing!

You get it, right? The good, bad, ugly, and fantastical—it's all here *for* you.

The Final Poems

For Real, It's Time

How quickly can I release
the little grip on my heart
notice from the start
if it's for me or not?

And that's really all it is
trusting the no
no judgment
just learning the language of my soul

I'm really good now
no longer stuck
in any chaotic muck
confusion is a sacred no

I love knowing the no
So clear; so obvious
I can't want something so much
and ignore the message

I don't ever have to guess
Nothing is ever really a test
It's only a matter
of paying close attention

My focus is key
with crystal clear seeing
my heart leads
and I can soar

Flying higher, faster, easier
every moment *for* me
to play, to dance, to sing
my soul song

I'll never get this wrong
from here on out
I'm out loud (she's here)
a magical alien superpowered goddess

There's no fear anymore
and all that's in store
is peace and ease
Please, naysayers. . .

. . . you can't.
You won't stop the fire
the wild words
I'm here to chant

Now, for real
it's time to be brave!

Take it Slow

I take the day slow
Hawk cries pull me outside
Ah, child of the sun
Spring has sprung, and
so has my life
a fun experiment of love
and loss
how to toss fear aside
and risk going for it all

Why not?
What, seriously, have I got to lose?

Am I to dance with cherry blossoms
under the light of moonrise
and forget anything is possible?

That life is a miracle?
And that I'm alive to inhale it?
That I'm alive for the soul purpose
of the ecstasy available?

Or am I to drown
in doubt
Always fearing, anxiety-ridden,
about to lose it
because I believe the lies?

Wake up. Question everything. Ask for help.
Miracles are waiting.

Take the day slow, my friends.
Remember who you are.

It Always Comes Back to You

It always comes back to you
Every time my soul comes out to play
she reminds me what to do

Standing before me like a mountain
a river of love
a silent wall of joy

You hold me easily in your arms
and never let go
You never let go first

Your smile burns through me
purple fire
us intertwined

Flowing yin and yang
barefoot on the sand
we're free

Nobody else needs to see
All we need is trust
All we need is us

Our hearts as witness
the only things to protect
It's how we heal everything

And I'm afraid to want it
afraid to ask
Time passes, and it's harder.

I'm afraid to tell you
how much this means
Feels like you're the air I breathe

Feels like if one day
you're not around
I'll lose everything I know about love

My soul is loud and clear
It's a now-or-never thing
I choose now

Moving fear aside
I step up to speak
no matter what

No matter if you think I'm a fool
I say the words and risk it all
Yeah, I'm a fool for bigger love.

Wounded Gorgeous Soul

Wounded soul
know your worth.
Your desperate cries
only make a deeper hole.
Your wrecked soul
will survive.
You were lovable
the moment we laid eyes on you.
You never had to say a word.
You never had to win.
You never had to try harder.
You never had to be anything else.
Anyone else.
Any better,
or smarter,
or prettier,
or luckier.

Wounded soul
you're a warrior.
Slay your doubt.
Use your fear as fuel.
The cruel words you hear
are coming from you.
Wake up.
Your desperate lies
only feed the wound.
Learn a new way.
Question the day you were taught
to hide,
never asking for what you truly desired,
never owning your truth,
never calling out their bullshit,
never standing up for yourself.

It's time to fill the cracks.
Sturdy the foundation.
Reinforce the launchpad with steel columns
of courage
from which your vision can be heard.
You were meant to heal the world,
wounded soul.
Every god and goddess has to train.
And you are the master someone's waiting for.
Realize your wound
is the gift
not the curse.
Scars are stronger than perfect skin.
Everything you've ever wanted
lies within the walls you've tried to build
so we wouldn't see the miracle that is you.

Wounded soul
you're perfect just as you are.
A star in the darkness.
Hope in a hopeless world.
The reason we can breathe.
Can't you see?
It's the wound that got you to the place
you can be everything you were meant to be.
The wound
is the freedom you seek.
It holds the key.
It always has.
You were never broken.
The most painful parts
were always the path
to the joy.
Wounded gorgeous soul.
I love you.
It's time to shine.

A Rampage of Gratitude

When poets gather, in all stages of I'm-not-sure-I'm-a-poet and raise their hands to be vulnerable and share anyway, my heart sings, and my purpose of brave healing becomes clear.

Each of the featured poets from all over the world did exactly that. Thank you, poets! Thank you for saying yes to this marvelous project, and for taking on my challenge of being vulnerable and trailblazing that strength for the world! Thanks for your passion for poetry. Thanks for your courage and kindness. You are amazing badasses. You are powerful healers. We keep poetry breathing and thriving because of you!

Kelly vdH Kaschula, thank you for the brilliant interior design, for being patient with my million revisions, and for always getting the mission of making the books more than a book!

Davide DeAngelis, thank you for the brilliant sunrise, for getting my colorful vision for our cover, and for being the one who can put my ideas into that visual form so brilliantly.

To the Brave Healer Productions team behind the scenes, every one of you who helps us complete every step of the process, thank you so much for believing in our mission and helping me take this company to the empire level it is.

To Dinahsta "Miss Kiane" Thomas, thank you for the mission you have with The InkWell and for inviting me into your poetry world to partner with you. Because of that partnership, love, and support, this book became way more than a book. You inspire me constantly, and you're part of the reason I will never give up on my own poetry.

To everyone who reads this book, thank you for your interest and passion for poetry or for your simple curiosity about what this book is about. If you were a part of our book launch team, on behalf of our entire poet cast, thank you so much! You are the reason these books and their brave words move out into the world in a much bigger way.

About the Lead Poet

Laura Di Franco is the CEO of Brave Healer Productions (including Brave Business Books and Brave Kids Books), an award-winning publisher for holistic health, wellness, and business professionals who want to become bestselling authors, build their community and business, and leave their legacy in a more conscious way.

She has a master's and 30 years of expertise in holistic physical therapy, is a third-degree black belt in Taekwondo, and is the author of 14 books. Brave Healer Productions has published over 100 Amazon bestselling books with a mission to help the world experience what's possible, one brave word at a time.

Laura is a divorced mom (of two adult kids and one dog), lover of the sunrise and dark chocolate, spoken-word poet, inspirational speaker, and is convinced she was a race car driver in a past life. She has a contagious passion for helping you share brave words that build your business and leave your legacy.

Join the community on Facebook in the Brave Badass Healers, a Community for World-Changers group, to enjoy free monthly business development and networking. Want some advice about your book idea? Schedule a chat with our publishing team!

Get access to *The Brave Healer Resources Vault* with training and masterclasses for author-entrepreneurs: https://lauradifranco.com/resources-vault/

Connect with Laura:

Website: https://BraveHealer.com

LinkedIn: https://www.linkedin.com/in/laura-di-franco-mpt-1b037a5/

YouTube:
https://www.youtube.com/c/BraveHealerProductionswithLauraDiFranco

YouTube for Poetry:
https://www.youtube.com/@positivelypurposefulpoetry8316

Other Poetry Books from Laura Di Franco and Brave Healer Productions

Warrior Love, a Journal to Inspire Your Fiercely Alive Whole Self

Warrior Joy, a Journal to Inspire Your Fiercely Alive Whole Self

Warrior Soul, a Journal to Inspire Your Fiercely Alive Whole Self

Warrior Dreams, a Journal to Inspire Your Fiercely Alive Whole Self

(The first four Warrior Journal projects were published
under my married name, Laura Probert)

Warrior Desire, Love Poems to Inspire Your Fiercely Alive Whole Self

Life Lines: Poetry for Your Soul

100 Poems & Possibilities for Healing Volume 1 & 2

Ready to publish your poetry in our next poetry book collaboration?
Reach out to the team at support@LauraDiFranco.com

Listen to the spoken word:

Positively Purposeful Poetry
https://www.youtube.com/@positivelypurposefulpoetry8316

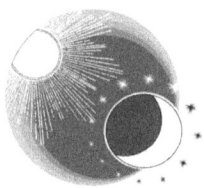

Dear reader, feel free to replace "Aquarian" with your birth sign in the following poem and read it out loud to yourself!

With big warrior love,
Laura

Good morning Aquarian sun
born to write and bask
on sun-warmed slopes carpeted with
dandelion fields
Any wish is your command

Stand tall today my alien friend
send messages of love like you do
and do not worry about those
who don't receive
You know who you are

Don't be anything else
for anyone's sake
You're already doing God's work
To pretend or shape yourself
into anything else would be the only mistake

Good morning Aquarian sun
Shine your brilliant golden light
The day you were born
was the day this world came alive
with the gift of you

Today is a day to celebrate
make firm your commitments
break every last habit of less
test the Universe
ask for everything you need

Vision, dream, and rest
in your power
taste peace nesting in your soul
receive it all and know
you're good today, and every day beyond this